JOB & JONAH

JOB & JONAH

Questioning
the
Hidden God

Bruce Vawter, C.M.

Paulist Press
new york/ramsey

Library of Congress
Catalog Card Number: 82-62413

ISBN: 0-8091-2524-2

Published by Paulist Press
545 Island Road, Ramsey, N.J. 07446

Printed and bound in the
United States of America

CONTENTS

In grateful memory of
Eugenio Pacelli,
Pope Pius XII,
and of the encyclical letter
Divino afflante Spiritu,
forty years after.
And of esteemed colleagues
who before and after
fought the good fight.
Eppur si muove.

FOREWORD

This is a small book, dealing with what some may think to be a small issue. Do the Books of Job and Jonah matter this much, these minority reports filed against the dominant religious orthodoxy of a tiny ethnic community in Palestine several centuries before the birth of Christ? They do matter, obviously, first of all because they are part of the Bible—and only a sophomoric mind, whatever its ideas or lack of them may be concerning the Bible's content and message, can pretend that the Bible does not matter. The Bible is not the oldest literature of the world, but it is unarguably the oldest still living literature that has done the most to shape the thought and development of those who have inhabited and do inhabit this world.[1] Specifically, though it may rightly be designated a cultural literature, what has rendered the Bible virtually unique among cultural literatures has been its character of not merely reflecting the society that produced it but of standing in judgment upon that society, thus bearing within itself the seeds of "sacred discontent," of dynamic growth, and change, and betterment.

Job and Jonah are preeminent examples of this judgmental character of the Bible. They begged to differ from the conventional wisdom that had evolved in postexilic Judaism as an important aspect of normative religion, a distillation of prophecy, law, and wisdom, with a touch of apocalypticism, which eventually emerged as Pharisaism, and which passed with some further Hellenistic modifications into the theological and ethical praxis of early Christianity. We must admire the catholic spirit of the orthodox rabbis who made the final decisions on the extent of the canon of the Hebrew Scrip-

1

tures and eventually certified recalcitrant works like these, not without great soul-searching.

If there is one thing that has been shown by the history of the canonical process, whether it was the process of the rabbis or of the early Church fathers, it is that the fathers were often wiser than their children have been in discerning what is the word of God. Further, they have often been wiser than many of their children in discerning what was and remains the purpose of the biblical message.

The biblical message is meant not only to console but to challenge and provoke. If one reads the Bible only to find comfort and consolation in fixed positions, the meaning of the Bible has been missed. Some "Bible-Christians" misunderstand the Bible precisely in this way: they search it for confirmation in their prejudices rather than for a summons to reexamine their premises. One is frequently awestruck at the confidence with which the nature and designs of God—which the Bible says in many respects are unknowable by us—are proclaimed plain as a pikestaff, down to some rather precise determinations about whom he has or has not decided to favor with heavenly life, and why. It is a confidence that makes the claims of the Roman Pontiff seem rather timid by comparison. A healthy dose of Job and Jonah, taken without prejudice and without concern for the frivolous non-issues that clutter up "conservative" commentaries, could put a dent in such confidence.

I am well aware that my interpretation of Job and Jonah, as regards both their place in time and their function in that time, will differ from that of others, on the quite respectable grounds of literary and historical criticism. If I do not always advert to opposed positions, it is not that I do not know them or that I make light of them. It has been task enough for me to offer the interpretation that persuades me, hoping that it will also persuade others.

This volume contains some notes. Reviewers of some of my previous books have noted the absence of notes as a defect. Though I am not convinced that the notes will contribute markedly to the enlightenment of the reader, I have decided to include them, and if they do help, so much the better.

Notes

1. See Herbert N. Schneidau, *Sacred Discontent. The Bible and Western Tradition* (Berkeley: University of California Press, 1976).

On the Usages

Schüler:	Fast möcht' ich nun Theologie studieren.
Mephistopheles:	Ich wünschte nicht, Euch irre zu führen.
	Was diese Wissenschaft betrifft,
	Es ist so schwer, den falschen Weg zu meiden,
	Es liegt in ihr so viel verborgnes Gift,
	Und von der Arzenei ist's kaum zu unterscheiden.
	Am besten ist's auch hier, wenn Ihr nur *Einen* hört,
	Und auf des Meisters Worte schwört.
	Im ganzen—haltet Euch an Worte!
	Dann geht Ihr durch die sichre Pforte
	Zum Tempel der Gewissheit ein.
Schüler:	Doch ein Begriff muss bei dem Worte sein.
Mephistopheles:	Schon gut! Nur muss man sich nicht allzu ängstlich quälen;
	Denn eben wo Begriffe fehlen,
	Da stellt ein Wort zur rechten Zeit sich ein.
	Mit Worten lässt sich trefflich streiten,
	Mit Worten ein System bereiten,
	An Worte lässt sich trefflich glauben,
	Von einem Wort lässt sich kein Iota rauben.

(J. W. v. Goethe, *Faust I,* 1982–2000)

4

of Theology

Student: Almost, then, theology would I try!
Mephisto: I would not like to see you stray thereby,
            For in this lore, to say no more than just,
            It is full hard to 'scape the wrongful track,
            Wherein's disclosed so much envenomed must:
            With magic arts you'll find it back to back.

            Here, too, *one* man's the wisest choice:

            Give heed to no one but the master's voice.
            In sum—stick to the verbal text.
            You'll find the temple gates quite next
            Where surety is shrined.
Student: But words should be the sounds of mind!
Mephisto: Right on! Yet where of thought there is a lack,

            Words have a way of closing up the slack.
            Thus, in such matters be not over vexed.
            With words we joust as though in chivalerie,
            With words we constitute philosophie,
            In words we noble creeds endower,
            Think not to rob the word of one jot of its power.

1.

WITHOUT MAN, THERE IS NO GOD

No mere literary conceit has prompted the introduction to this book of Mephisto's gently cynical observations on the ways of theology. In the "Heavenly Prologue" to *Faust* Goethe has designed a scene obviously modeled on Job 1:6–12. Here the "sons of God" who assemble as dutiful courtiers before the divine throne are the angels Raphael, Gabriel, and Michael, the only three whose names were "known" through the Jewish–Christian canon of the Old Testament books. Unlike the unnamed and voiceless sons of God of the Job story, however, these are vocal indeed. They paean, successively, the praise of a creator God who has ordered all things well, whose world is the mirror of his perfection, since seas and sun and earth and every natural thing still go their lordly way as when they first were made. Theirs is a hymn to the deist's God, the architect of the universe.

As in Job, so in *Faust* it is the Satan/Mephistopheles who shatters this idyllic phantasm. And with precisely the same objection. For how can God be complacent about his world as long as the man whom he made god upon earth is in total disharmony with his destiny? To the Lord's exasperated cry,

On earth can you find nothing ever rightful?

Mephisto's reply is,

Nay, Lord! As always, I find it truly frightful.

7

So much men brook in rounding out their daily plot,
Not even I have heart to further plague this wretched lot.

It is true, neither the Mephistopheles of *Faust* nor the Satan of Job has understood either God or man. That bit of irony is part of the genius of both the biblical and the German poet. But—and this, too, is the genius of the two poets—it is the tempter, the dissenter, the trickster who has been permitted to raise the crucial question and objection. Mephisto and the Satan are personifications of the restless human mind, a mind whose nature it is to question and to ask. This human mind, conceived in the image and likeness of God according to the insight of the Book of Genesis, is the essential complement of God himself. There is no God, in any meaningful sense of the word, unless he is understood by men. Man is the only of his creatures to whom it has been given to *know* God, in however diluted a fashion, even as God knows man. The New Testament would later say, in deprecation of the Old, that no one had ever seen (= known) God (John 1:18), in spite of the many Old Testament passages which speak of God as both seen and known and in spite of the prophets' charge against Israel that it was culpable precisely because it had refused to acknowledge the God whom it had known (Isa 1:3–4; Hos 4:1–6, etc.).

What this means, of course, is that knowledge, a human attainment, is, as we know very well, conditioned by and relative to the human person as he exists in an historical process whose beginning we imperfectly grasp, in which we now consist, and whose end we can only gropingly conjecture. By the same token the knowledge of God, also a human attainment, is subject to the same inexorable rules. In his *Summa theologiae,* Thomas Aquinas makes it the foundation of his theology that, even when enlightened by grace, man in this life can never know God "as he is": he can only bow to the law of his sense-directed mind and imagine a God who possesses eminently the perfections he perceives imperfectly realized in himself and in other creatures with none of their concomitant defects (*Prima pars,* q. 12, art. 12–13; q. 13, art. 2–3).

In the first chapter of Genesis, a work which is tributary to many centuries of religious experience and reflection, there is the grand pronouncement that man, mankind, male and female, has been created in the image and likeness of God. This is, on the one hand, an act of sublime faith, flung in the teeth of an experience of man that was totally without illusion. The man of Gen 1:27 is, after all, man mythically conceived as a prior to this experience, man with all his history peeled away, man as he ideally should be. (Not, be it noted, man as he once was: there is no evidence that the biblical mythology historicized its tales in quite so crass a fashion.) How vile man could be, when he set himself to the task, certainly came as no bit of information of which the authors of the Old Testament were innocent.

What makes Gen 1:27 so interesting is, in fact, that it tells us less about men, whom the authors of Genesis knew warts and all, than it does about God, whose nature they could only imagine. There is no way around it: For man God *is* man—ideal man—writ large. In this perspective God is the pious Jew who works a six-day week at creation and rests, as pious Jews should, on the seventh day. He is the God who imposes on Abraham (Genesis 17) the covenant of circumcision, a practice which was doubtless ancient in the Semitic world, but which became a matter of religious orthodoxy only in postexilic times. God is represented, here and elsewhere, as concerned about the most minute details of ritual and cultural law and custom. Such details were essential to the preservation of Jewish identity in the postexilic community, however irrelevant they must appear to many readers of Genesis today. That identity then included the harsh measures of Ezra and Nehemiah against marriages with Gentiles (Ezra 9; Neh 13:23–31) and the total for ever exclusion from membership in the community of God's people of such mongrel nations as the Ammonites and Moabites—people like you and me— even though with them Israel acknowledged ethnic kinship (see Deut 23:4). The harshness of such measures did not prevail without contemporary opposition: witness the Book of Ruth, which portrays a pious Moabitess adhering to the ancient ways of Israel and becoming in the event an essential ancestress of the great King David! But it did prevail, to preserve the (largely fictitious) purity of Israel's blood-lines, and in the process it determined for generations the image of God.

What we say is that by "God" we, like those who have gone before us, simply try to give a name to the meaning and rationale of our existence in this world. That is all that Aquinas was trying to say. Nowadays some might prefer to substitute a "what" for the "who" of the God of Aquinas' syllogisms. The difference is not as radical a departure as might at first be thought. Any sophisticated believer must recognize at some state that in God there is neither sex nor gender, that it is as natural, though less usual, for us of the "West" to ascribe to God feminine characteristics as it is to ascribe masculine ones. Just as natural, and just as inadequate. The Bible stands accused in our times of masculine bias and of a proclivity for "sexist" language. The accusation is lodged with some justice, for there is no denying that the Bible, Old Testament and New, is the product of a thoroughly male-oriented culture, a culture which assumed such an orientation quite unself-consciously and to which any other would have seemed strange and forced. Such an orientation and its resultant language cannot, ultimately, be removed from the Bible through translational artifices without damage to the Bible's integrity as historical witness. They are, in any case, only one of the outer edges of the greater stumbling block which is the Bible itself.[1]

The metaphor "word of God" which we apply to the Bible is precisely that, a metaphor and not a strict definition. We speak far more univocally when we admit to the obvious fact that the Bible is the word of man, of man touched—so faith informs us—by divine grace, but at all events of man throughout. Were this not so, there would be no point in our critically restoring biblical texts in our pursuit of comparative philology, the data supplied by archeology and ancient epigraphy and all those disciplines which are aimed at reconstituting a culturally and historically conditioned human psyche at the moment of biblical composition—all of which no one will contest is necessary in determining the Bible's "literal sense." For the believer, the Bible is indeed the word of God, but mediately so, through the word of man. More accurately put, the Bible is the word of man in which the word of God may be heard. Here we collide with the notorious ambiguity of our English "word," mirror of the equally ambiguous *dabar* or *logos* that it translates, which occupies some fourteen columns in the *Oxford English Dictionary,* and which so very often is cavalier in its treatment of the "words" by which it is conveyed. Not only the biblical but every word is subject to this ambivalence and polyvalence. Language and words need not be only informative or aimed at cognition; they may be performative, expressive, take on cohesive or other functions incapable of being captured by dictionary definitions.[2]

We have referred to the Bible as a stumbling block, which is merely to say that it is a *skandalon* in the Pauline sense (Rom 9:33, 1 Cor 1:23, Gal 5:11), that is, a thing, an event, a personage, in itself profane, commonplace, even ludicrous, in which faith alone can perceive a transcendent significance. The people who are called and who sometimes call themselves fundamentalists make the mistake of trying to dissolve this *skandalon* when they speak of the Bible as "self-authenticating" and pronounce its word to be "infallible" or "inerrant"—terms which are not only unbiblical but also profoundly anti-biblical. James Barr, who has recently written wisely if not altogether charitably about the phenomenon of fundamentalism,[3] has correctly noted that the "literalism" of which the fundamentalist is supposed to be guilty in his approach to the Bible is actually the farthest thing from his mind. More often the fundamentalist flees from the literal sense of the Bible, distorts, denies, or transforms it, in service to his gratuitous assumption that the Bible must not contradict presently known scientific or historical fact or betray itself with any inner incoherence. This unhistorical and mythical concept of the Bible as an oracular compendium of any and all knowledge is a modern superstition that has only tenuous connections with the Judaism and Christianity from which it has sprung and which it has totally misunderstood.

The Bible, as a gathering of ancient oriental literary material, is neither inerrant nor infallible, nor is it internally cohesive in every respect. Therein lies its *skandalon,* and therein consists its perennial fascination. Its scientific information is, to put it most charitably, rudimentary and primitive, understandably so as the product of a pre-scientific age, rendered comic only when pressed into the service of such excursions into wrongheadedness as go by names like that of "creationism." Its history is frequently accurate, frequently approximative, mingled with myth and legend, and always tendentious. Its history is sometimes even a revisionism of a type not unlike that of the *Great Soviet Encyclopaedia,* in which what ought to have been, according to the received ideology, is deliberately substituted for what actually was. The Bible disagrees with itself even—especially—

in affirmations touching on the veriest essentials of biblical faith. When the Second Vatican Council decreed that Sacred Scripture teaches "firmly, faithfully, and without error the truth which God wanted put into the sacred writings for the sake of our salvation,"[4] it enunciated a true saying worthy of all men to be believed. But it was speaking of Sacred Scripture, of the Bible not as a collection of disparate human documents but rather as a normative canon of sacred literature whose meaning had been determined by as much as it had determined the experience of God's people, specifically the church. It said nothing about specific texts or books or authors whose efforts underlie what eventually emerged as the canon of Sacred Scripture.

The Bible, in its wrestling with the God question, indulges nothing that is petty or banal. The psalmist who wrote (Pss 14:1; 55:2), "The fool says in his heart, 'There is no God,' " meant only to observe that there is a great number of unthinking people who act as though there were no standard higher than their own appetites and whims to dictate the course of their conduct. This is an ethical statement, not an affirmation of theodicy. Why bother to question the "theoretical" existence of Chemosh of the Moabites if, indeed, for the Moabites Chemosh really "worked" as an imperative deity? Or Baal for the Canaanites? Or Melkart for the Syrians? The Israelites knew, in their better moments at least, that Yahweh of Israel was indeed a God who "worked," and their rejection of the gods of the Gentiles as "false" was not to call into question their theoretical existence—a matter of undeniable human conception—but rather their practical efficacy, their inability to perform the deeds which their clients ascribed to them. Doctrinaire atheism, a modern fundamentalist reaction to fundamentalist theism, was unknown to the psalmist. He would have regarded it as a perverse refusal to give a name to ideals which were and are otherwise passionately worshiped.

John Garvey has recently put very well what is the real question, the question in which the Bible is really interested:

> We ordinarily make a sharp distinction between belief and non-belief, perhaps allowing for gray areas in between. Maybe the division should be done differently, between those who are easy in their belief or non-belief, and those who see agony in either place. In this sense Madalyn Mur-

ray O'Hair and Jerry Falwell have a lot in common; so do Pascal and Camus. The great questions are the ones conventional believers and non-believers are often relaxed about. Does the fact that we are alive matter? What evidence do we have for a loving God—for that matter, what evidence is there that God is even vaguely decent?[5]

It is these great questions of agony that are the questions of the Bible. We shall see, in the following pages, just a few of them, raised in a moment of time whose external history we know but imperfectly, a time of whose anguish and doubt we are abundantly informed, relieved and illumined as they were by the sardonic humor with which men of faith have often mocked themselves for failing to expect the unexpected from a Lord of the absurd whose ways are not their own.

Notes

1. A point which, I feel, is overlooked, with some consequent bad conclusions, in an article with which it is otherwise hard to disagree, by Gail Ramshaw Schmidt, "De Divinibus Nominibus: The Gender of God," *Worship* 56 (1982) 117–131.

2. G. B. Caird, *The Language and Imagery of the Bible* (Philadelphia: Westminster, 1980) 7–36.

3. *Fundamentalism* (Philadelphia: Westminster, 1978).

4. Walter M. Abbott, S.J., *The Documents of Vatican II* (New York: Guild Press, 1966) 119.

5. *Commonweal* 108 (1981) 300, at the beginning of a review article entitled "The Gnostics Among Us."

2.

A BEST AND WORST
OF WORLDS

What is a best and worst of all possible worlds—one that could respond to the litany of good and ill that Dickens has mingled in his first paragraph of *A Tale of Two Cities*? Undoubtedly, it is every age in which we mortals have been destined to dwell, ever since history began, which is when man thought it worthwhile to remember and record. In our Christian history "the age of faith" was indeed that of Aquinas, Bonaventure, Albertus Magnus, Roger Bacon, Dante, Prester John; and also that of Innocent III, the Albigenses and the Cathari, of the Children's Crusade and of abysmal superstition. The following century, by Barbara Tuchman termed "calamitous,"[1] was the age of Wycliffe and Huss, and also of the "Babylonian captivity" of the papacy and of the Black Death, an unspeakable plague propagated by ignorance which decimated Europe and, more seriously, in its wake propagated even more unspeakable crimes against the image of God in man. The fifteenth and sixteenth centuries gave us—let us name them only, without prejudice—Reformation and Counter-Reformation, Thomas à Kempis, François Villon, the abbey of Thélème, the Peasants' Revolt, the Wars of Religion, and Alexander VI's bisecting of a terrestrial globe to satisfy equally the colonial appetites of Spain and Portugal. The Enlightenment, finally, which sparked both the American and the French revolutions, which gave birth to Voltaire, the Encyclopedists, and the enthronement of Reason, also was midwife to the Terror and to the greatest ever traffic in human

14

slavery, sanctioned now not only by religion but also by newly discovered science.

For the moment, let us pass over our own and recent ages and concentrate our attention on that period with which we shall be concerned in this book. We are talking about the great débâcle that had overtaken Judah, that tiny Near Eastern pocket of a peculiar Yahwistic religion and polity, toward the end of the sixth century B.C.

The fall of the Northern Kingdom [of Israel] shook Judah to its foundations, as seen from the prophecies of Isaiah and Micah and the subsequent reformation under Josiah (640–609 B.C.). Zephaniah, Jeremiah, Habakkuk, and Ezekiel were genuinely alarmed by the flouting of the covenant under Jehoiakim (609–597 B.C.) and Zedekiah (598–587 B.C.). Jeremiah especially counseled submission to the yoke of Babylon as punishment for the nation's deviation (Jer 32, 26–35).

The first onslaught of Nebuchadnezzar in 597 B.C. should have been ample warning to the authorities to mend their ways, but it only made them more wilfully resistant to the admonitions of the prophets, and matters grew worse. The headlong plunge toward disaster was not to be halted; in fact, it was to be accelerated in direct proportion to the application of political pressure from without and prophetic exhortation from within. The outside pressures were exerted, on the one hand, by Babylon, which demanded loyalty on the part of its vassal state, and on the other hand, by the princes of Moab, Ammon, Edom, Tyre, and Sidon (Jer 27), who did everything in their power to incite revolt against Babylon, probably at the instigation of Egypt (Jer 37), which was ever ready to create a disturbance without getting too deeply involved. Jeremiah counselled loyalty to Babylon (27, 12–15) but was opposed by rulers and religious officials (27, 16ff.). The more Jeremiah exhorted the nation to accept the yoke of Babylon as the will of Yahweh, the more frantically active became his opponents—all of which hastened the day of reckoning. Even after the final blow had fallen on Jerusalem [Nebuchadnezzar's sack of the city and destruction of its Temple in 587/6], certain groups remaining in the land refused to accept the situation and continued the struggle against the inevitable (see Jer 41–44).[2]

This evocation of the remote Judahite past might seem to contain a message for our own recent past, but we shall forgo at this moment any attempt to exploit the parallel. Suffice it for our purposes to stick to the ineluctable historical facts. We are not dealing, as we might be tempted to deal, with a backward, "emerging," "third-world" ex-colonial state of ill-educated and ill-equipped leadership suddenly thrust on the stage of world events and offered the choice of either allying itself with one of the two superpowers of its then world or of pursuing a policy of "non-alignment" which is in reality a firm alignment on a very definite side. Judah's leaders may have toyed with such fantasies when they were in a position to do something with them. They no longer enjoyed any such position.

Jerusalem and Judah—the sacred land—and the temple—the sacred place of Yahweh's dwelling which had joined every subsequent generation to the already legendary age of David and Solomon—these were gone. Gone, and with them gone the religious and national wellsprings that had watered and nourished Israelite identity for centuries. The people that had called itself the darling[3] of the gods, the chosen of Yahweh the very God, now found itself outcast and rootless. Rootlessness was then, as it now is, a summons and a challenge to the human soul to bring forth the worst and yet the best of what it can conceive and do. And, then as it does now, it conceived and did everything both evil and good, with a great deal of the indifferent in between, all the way from mindless violence and dementia through apathy and cynicism to its noblest possible aspirations for new purpose and new direction.

The summons and challenge were, in this instance, further complicated by a factor that had once been Israel's glory and now could so remain, a bedrock for faith, but also could be the proverbial stone of stumbling. That factor was prophecy. The preexilic prophets, from Amos through Jeremiah, had foretold the doom that would inexorably descend upon Israel and Judah for all their manifold sins against God and man. The doom had descended, and no one could doubt it. So much was prophecy vindicated. But Jeremiah, who had—despite every fibre of his being that yearned for peace with his fellowman—counseled the hotspurs of his generation to bow to the yoke of the king of Babylon (27:1–11), who had written to the first exiles in Babylon instructing them to reconcile themselves to their fate, to settle in this alien land and discover their destiny there (29:1–15)—this same Jeremiah couples with these prophetic words other words of assurance that at the end of this exile, which would last for a symbolic seventy years (29:10), there would be a complete restoration when all would be as before, Israel secure again upon its own soil and with its own institutions intact.[4] (Centuries later, the author of Daniel 9, confronted by the harsh historical realities that had apparently demonstrated Jeremiah's vision to have been somewhat more than cloudy, could reconcile with these realities his faith in prophecy only by assuming that the prophet must have been contemplating not seventy years but seventy *weeks* of years.) Ezekiel, too, who had spared neither Israel nor Judah nor his fellow exiles in Babylonia the lash of his bitter, often crude and grotesque taunts as the words of a vengeful God, had nevertheless foreseen and foretold an almost impossibly ideal future in which the Israel that had been and the Judah that was nearly not would once more be united under the Davidic monarchy of yore (Ezek 37:15–28, for example).[5] This notion of a reunification of an Israel scattered among the nations was dear to exilic and postexilic prophets who annotated the works of their contrary predecessors to bring them into line (cf. Amos 9:11–15; Mic 2:12–13, 4:6–7, etc.), a line, unfortunately, that was to lead nowhere. And what, finally, of that greatest of the exilic prophets, the one whom we know as the Second Isaiah, whose Book of Consolation (Isaiah 40–55) had promised everlasting peace and tranquillity for a redeemed Israel, a Zion crowned with everlasting joy toward which all the nations of the earth would beat their way, over a highway for which mountains would be leveled and valleys raised, that all might see the glory of the Lord?

The Chronicler, the postexilic historian whose work we know as 1–2 Chronicles plus Ezra and Nehemiah, was certainly a revisionist in his use of sources, most of which, though not necessarily all, he extracted from the Pentateuch and the Deuteronomical History (Genesis–Deuteronomy; Joshua–2 Kings): works which for him already possessed some quality of "canonical" status. In his use of Ezra and Nehemiah, which were certainly of such recent vintage as to have no patina of canonicity, he has, however, permitted certain brute facts to make their presence ineluctably known, even though these too he arranged in a fashion best suited to his ends.

Both 2 Chr 36:22–23 and Ezra 1:1–4 record a decree of Cyrus the Persian, conqueror of the Babylon that had conquered Judah, permitting the Jews in exile to return to Jerusalem and rebuild there their temple of the Lord. There is no reason to question the accuracy of the record, which is in accord with known Persian policy. Nothing less had been expected of Cyrus by the Second Isaiah, who had recognized in him the coming world conqueror (Isa 41:25) who would also be the Lord's chosen ruler, his servant, his messiah, the restorer of his people and of their religion in the land (Isa 44:28–45:1).

Nevertheless, the realization was far less romantic than the anticipation. Among the first to return was Sheshbazzar, "the prince of Judah" (Ezra 1:8). He may be the Shenazzar of 1 Chr 3:18. Obviously he was a Davidic descendant, and just as obviously he bore an authentic Babylonian name. We hear no more of him. Next appears Zerubbabel the son of Shealtiel, another Davidide (1 Chr 3:19). Aside from his being given credit for the foundation of the Second Temple (Ezra 3), Zerubbabel, too, speedily disappears from the Chronicler's history. We can only suspect what happened, since our factual knowledge of the age is far from satisfactory. The nationalist prophets Haggai and Zechariah who were among the returnees from Babylonia joined to their exhortations for the immediate rebuilding of the temple an equally urgent call for the restoration of the Davidic monarchy (cf. Hag 1:1–2, 2:20–23; Zech 4–6). The Achaemenid Persian empire was, by the standards of its time (or of any time, for that matter), benign and tolerant of deviant and alien religions and folkways within its hegemony, pluralistic and ecumenical. But it could not sustain a rival monarchy of even modest pretensions within this hegemony, and therefore it must have crushed it and obliterated it utterly and without trace. So much for the Davidic prince who would preside over the new people Israel (Jer 33:14–17; Amos 9:11–15, etc.).

We have remarked on the Babylonian name of Sheshbazzar. It is a note equally to be remarked of Zerubbabel ("one born in Babylon"), of course. One word at least of Jeremiah that the exiles in Babylonia had accepted was his injunction that they become assimilated into this land (Jer 29:1–7). (That doctrine, within a few years, would become an anathema to Ezra and Nehemiah.) Ezra 8 is one indication of what beating of the bush—at whatever time is to be proposed in the notoriously vexed Ezra-Nehemiah chronology—was necessary to persuade Jews of the diaspora to "return" to Zion. These were people who, even within a few short decades, had settled into a new land, assimilated its genius, and become members of its *Gemeinschaft,* its human community. So it had been with the Marashu brothers, descendants of second-class citizens or worse, who eventually reached a pinnacle of commercial power in Persian Babylon.[6] And so, of course, it has been with the Fuggers and the Rothschilds. Jews of any age are no different from other people except to the extent that they have willed it so and others have willed it so. So much for ethnic identity.

The little territory of Yehud (Judah) to which the Babylonian exiles were invited to return was a tiny province of the Persian empire, perhaps twenty miles north and south by twenty-five east and west, surrounded on every side by equally subservient provinces, though each of greater size, which memorialized in their names and in their acts ancient enmities and bitter reminders of the past: Samaria, Ammon, Idumea (Edom), Ashdod, and the rest (cf. Neh 2:10, 19). Yehud—paradoxically, it is from this shrunken vestige of vanished Israelite glory that for the first time the survivors of the ancient covenant with Yahweh become properly known by the proud name they have ever after borne: *Yehudim,* the Jews. So much for a world dominion that would reign from sea to sea.

Enemies without and enemies within. So much for prophecies which had envisioned eternal peace, a people faithful to a law of God written on their hearts, and a Jerusalem to which the nations of the world would flock for solace and instruction in the ways of God. To be sure, a disinterested historian would have to conclude that these first Zionist Jews created their own problems and enmities, or at least did little to prevent them. The "people of the land" whom the Chronicler simply writes off as "enemies of Judah and Benjamin" appear to have been initially favorable and welcoming to the immigrants from Babylonia, eager to join with them in a common worship of Yahweh, only to find their overtures haughtily spurned and rebuffed (Ezra 3:3, 4:1–5). Who were these "people of the land"? Partly, indeed, what the Chronicler claims that they were, foreigners who had been transported into Palestine from other subject territories in keeping with the Assyrian policy of discouraging revolt by diluting native populations. But also, probably in greater part, they were simply the residual populace of the Palestine of Israelite times, common folk whose humble state had warranted no interference or deportation by the Chaldean conquerors a generation before. It is these, without doubt, who are responsible for the beautiful poetry of the Book of Lamentations, among other compositions that have found their way into the Hebrew Bible. In any case, foreigner or native, all these "people of the land" were Yahwists, fellow religionists with the Zionists, and their rejection by the latter can hardly be viewed as other than an act of doctrinaire chauvinism.

Similarly the Samaritans. The census list of the returnees from Babylonia (Ezra 2, but more properly in place at Nehemiah 7) includes Judahites, Jerusalemites, priests and other personnel of the temple. In conformity with the Chronicler's perspective, in which the northern kingdom of Israel was an embarrassment better left unspoken, Judah, Benjamin, and their appendages are all. The Israel of the north, nevertheless, had remained on Palestinian soil a Yahwistic people, despite the loss of their autonomy and political leadership through Assyrian tyranny. Now they were the Persian province of Samaria, governed by a Sanballat (Neh 2:10) who was evidently a faithful Yahwist.[7] Though the circumstances are obscure, it is doubtless from this time that we should date the beginnings of the celebrated hostility between Jew and Samaritan so apparent in the New Testament, a hostility that probably owed more to atavistic Judah vs. Israel political hatred than it did to religious principle. By the Jews the Samaritans came to be despised as a mongrel, degenerate people, less worthy of concern than the Edomites and the uncircumcised Philistines (cf. Sir 50:25–26). The irony is, of course, that northern Israel had first instituted all the great developments of Yahwism, political and religious, and that Judah had been a recent convert, only tardily assimilated into the kerygmatic history. But it is not unusual for the recent convert to recast history as though it began only with his conversion, or, rather, as though there were no conversion and instead he had been present at the creation.

Other events occurred of which we have much less than perfect knowledge. What of Tobiah the Ammonite "slave" (read, "servant of the king," just as Nehemiah was: Neh 2:10, etc.)? His name ("Yahweh is my good," or "Yahweh is the Good") proclaims him to have been a Yahwist, and he obviously held an exalted position in Israelite society (Neh 13:5) prior to his inability to demonstrate the purity of his bloodlines (Ezra 2:60; Neh 7:62). Was it Tobiah or was it Nehemiah who was responsible for the enmity and hostility? Even more Byzantine machinations were involved in the postexilic resettlement and reconstitution, if we may credit the plausible reconstruction which Margaret Barker has made of the process that went into the establishment of the new Israel.[8]

The cataloguing of bloodlines was, as we have already suggested, quite as contrived a procedure as that by which the *nouvel arrivé* of the present day is supplied, on order, with a noble genealogy and "coat of arms." The genealogies of Chronicles illustrate the point, dictated as they are by theology rather than by any genuine historical recollection. Theology dictated that every clan and family acceptable to the new establishment—including especially the Judahite and related clans which were actually late-comers into the Israelite federation—be endowed with a direct descent from one of the eponymous ancestors of the twelve tribes, that priests and levites be distributed in the land according to Deuteronomic law (elaborated within the cultural cocoon of the exile), and so forth.

We noted above that the Book of Ruth, written about this time,[9] cut through this flimflammery by presenting as its heroine a worthy woman who became the ancestress of the great King David, despite the fact that she was a Moabite who through the law of Deut 23:4, certified by Neh 13:1, could never enter into the community of Israel. Ruth, like the Books of Judith and Tobit, looks back to an earlier, more relaxed time of Israelite freedom that had been innocent of the regimented orthodoxy of Ezra and Nehemiah.

Yet we must also acknowledge that the "orthodox" works of the Hebrew canon—the works without which there would, indeed, be no canon at all—derive from this same time. Besides the Deuteronomic history and the history of the Chronicler which we have already mentioned, there were both essential elements of the Old Testament like Isaiah 24–27, works mainly of redaction like the Psalter, "the songbook of the Second Temple," and works which combined redaction with creativity, like the collection of snippets and commentary which eventually became the Book of Jeremiah[10] and, for that matter, the entire prophetic corpus of the Hebrew Bible of which, in a way, the Book of Jeremiah is paradigmatic.

For the most part, however, this was a period not of new inspiration but rather of anthologizing the old. It was not yet so bereft of confidence of possessing the spirit of God (contrast Paul in 1 Cor 7:40!) that it could sigh for the loss of prophecy as the loss of religious initiative and think to find it regained only through some new and wholly unexpected dispensation of the Lord (so 1 Macc 4:46, 9:27, 14:41), during which interim men must find their own way without the help of God. Though prophecy had disappeared, there were those who felt its creative spirit had, in God's designs, descended upon Israel's "wisdom" tradition and its sages.[11] Proverbs 1–9, the work of an author who collected into one a distillation of the best of Israel's contributions to the world's "wisdom,"[12] propounded this thesis. Wisdom was, at the outset, simply the observations of common sense which, of course, are usually to be successfully sought for only from men of quite uncommon sense, the sages. The sages formed an international community or fraternity, just as wise men do today, cutting across national, religious, and cultural boundaries. The sages were less the philosophers of the day than they were the pragmatic counselors, though their counsel was generally empirically sound and reflective as well as pious. Wisdom was conceded to be an international import into Israel, with earlier origins in Egypt and Edom (Job!), for example (cf. 1 Kgs 5:10–11; Jer 49:7), and, in fact, it seems to be fairly proven that generous parts of Egyptian wisdom have served as models for Israelite aphorisms.[13] At the same time, and possibly for the same reason, the counsel of the wise with its appeal to *le bon sens* was frequently anathema to the free spirit of prophecy (cf. Isa 3:3, 19:11, 29:14, 31:2).

In the absence of prophecy and in the headiness of its own inheritance, wisdom in Proverbs 8 proclaims itself to be the rationale of the universe, the principle upon which God has created all that is, and therefore the way by which men may find God. This presupposes a sublime ideal, that the human mind can indeed penetrate into the divine. It is the basis of theology, which is traditionally defined as *fides quaerens intellectum,* belief which is looking for a rational justification. The justification was accepted by the author of the Wisdom of Solomon (who went on to assimilate Hellenistic wisdom into his essentially Jewish faith) and by Ben Sira, who made wisdom the Torah itself (Sirach 24; also Baruch 3:9–4:4), but it was equally rejected by Job 28, not to mention the rest of Job, by Ecclesiastes, and by other sources.

There is no doubt, Ezra and Nehemiah—in whatever order—produced a lasting society that would never cease—that has never ceased—since its inception. It was combined of the same kind of disparate bits and pieces that have gone into the creation of any lasting society. For many it sufficed and does now suffice. It sufficed in varying degrees and with specific reservations and modifications, then as it does now. *Kashruth* and keeping a safe distance from the *goyim,* the ideal of the Book of Daniel, is the presupposition of the romantic idylls of Judith and Tobit. Purity in the face of God and man. No one can read the Book of Sirach, and especially its chapter 50:1–24, without recognizing in its gallant and comfortably aged author an estimable human being for whom God was manifest completely not only in his revealed law which was the rule of life but also in the liturgy of the Second Temple whereby he became as visibly present as he had been to the prophet Isaiah (Isaiah 6).

For others, however, it did not suffice, for they felt that the sources of inspiration had dried up, leaving an aching void that had not been filled and whose lack of fulfillment countenanced doubt, perplexity, and unease over simple solutions and glib orthodoxy. Prophecy had disappeared. Its place had been usurped by wisdom, but wisdom, we have said, was faulted by some of its own practitioners. In the following chapters we propose to treat as examples of the creative disillusionment of the unsatisfied of this age a mild parody of prophecy that was carried out by the author of the Book of Jonah and a rather more thoroughgoing repudiation of the claims of wisdom that was produced by the author of the Book of Job.

good

Notes

1. *A Distant Mirror: The Calamitous 14th Century* (New York: Knopf, 1978).

2. J. M. Myers, *The World of the Restoration* (Englewood Cliffs: Prentice-Hall, 1968) 2–3.

3. The probable meaning of the *Jeshurun* of Isaiah 44:2. This poetic title for Israel seems to have been old, as indicated by the archaic poetry of Deut 32:15, 33:5.26.

4. It has long been recognized that chaps. 27–29 of Jeremiah form a distinct redactional unit characterized by its own vocabulary and style. Cf. B. N. Wambacq, O. Praem., *Jeremia* (De Boeken van het Oude Testament, 10; Roermond: Romen & Zonen, 1957) 179–180; Wilhelm Rudolph, *Jeremia* (HzAT 12; Tübingen: Mohr, 1958) 157–158. Neither can this entity be separated from the ultimate redaction of the Book of Jeremiah; cf. Winfried Thiel, *Die deuteronomistische Redaktion von Jeremia 26–45* (WMANT 52; Neukirchen-Vluyn: Neukirchener Verlag, 1981). There is, in any case, no reason to doubt that the passages cited do indeed represent authentic Jeremian words.

5. How much of the grandiose eschatological vision of chaps. 40–48 is Ezekiel's and how much is the result of later enthusiastic imitation can be debated. The substance is probably Ezekiel's.

6. Cf. H. Cazelles, "Murashu," *Dictionnaire de la Bible Supplément* 5, 1399; cf. 1, 797–8.

7. Cf. Roland de Vaux, O.P., *Ancient Israel* (New York: McGraw-Hill, 1961) 240, 242.

8. "The Two Figures in Zechariah," *Heythrop Journal* 18 (1977) 38–46; "The Evil in Zechariah," *ib.* 19 (1978) 12–27.

9. In his fine commentary on the Book of Ruth (*Ruth* [AB 7; Garden City: Doubleday, 1975]), Edward E. Campbell, Jr. suggests (pp. 23–28) an early rather than a late date for the composition of this book. His arguments are sound; but when he states that "Ruth is anything but a polemical piece," I feel that he has overlooked the most devastating form of polemics that consists in understatement and implication. I find it much easier to imagine Ruth composed to combat the legalism of Deut 23:4 and Neh 13:1 than to think that these latter were enacted by Davidic enthusiasts familiar with an ancient legend that had traced David's ancestry from a Moabitess (Campbell favors Ruth 4:17b as original to the book).

10. Cf. Thiel, as above.

11. Paul van Imschoot, "L'esprit de Jahvé, source de vie, dans l'Ancien Testament," *Revue biblique* 44 (1935) 481–501.

12. Cf. Patrick W. Skehan, "A Single Editor for the Whole Book of Proverbs," *Catholic Biblical Quarterly* 10 (1948) 115–130 (= [revised] *Studies in Israelite Poetry and Wisdom* [CBQMS 1; Washington, D.C.: Catholic Biblical Association, 1971] 15–26).

13. See, for example, the *New American Bible* footnote to Proverbs 22:19.

3.

THE LEGEND OF THE PATIENT JOB

Job 1:1 Once there was in the land of Uz a man by the name of Job. A perfect and upright man was he, godfearing and eschewing
2 evil. There were born to him seven sons and three daughters.
3 He also possessed seven thousand sheep, three thousand camels, and five hundred yoke of oxen, as well as five hundred she-asses and a host of retainers. He was the most important of all the men of the East.
4 It was his sons' custom to keep festival in each one's house by turns, to which they invited their three sisters to eat and drink
5 with them. And whenever their feasting days were over, then Job would send to have them purified, and he would make haste to offer sacrifices for each one of them. For, Job said, "maybe my sons have sinned and misspoken God in their hearts." So Job was wont to do always.

It is a celebrated question: Whether the prose introduction and conclusion to the Book of Job constitute an old folk tale that was taken over by the author of the poetic work which is most of the book, or is the same author also responsible for the prose story. The answer is, probably: neither the one nor the other but a bit of both. There is reason to believe, as we shall see, that the story had a literary history and development of its own independent of the poetry. There are also, as we shall see, indications that the prose has been tailored by the author of the poetry to suit his message and the use he has made of the Job legend.

Job—the name is ancient and common Semitic—was doubtless the subject of venerable folklore. In Ezek 14:14, 20 he appears, along with Noah and Daniel, as one of a triad of proverbially righteous men whose impetration and sacrifice were sufficient to atone for the sins of many and to please God. (Though in the case of sinful Israel, says Ezekiel, so great is their sin that not all three together could obtain such a reconciliation.) It is worthy of note, perhaps, that these three worthies were recalled not merely as saviors certain and sure, but also precisely as they were non-Israelites.

Noah we know, of course, as the survivor of the Flood, for whose sake not only an entire generation but mankind itself had been saved and who had, the Yahwist author believed, offered a sacrifice which atoned for a sinful race and, being accepted, marked a new relationship between God and man (Gen 8:20–22).[1] He was, equally, not an Israelite but rather the ancestor of all existing mankind, alike of the accursed Hamites and the tolerated Japhethites as well as of the Semites from which, eventually, Israel sprang. Daniel—he is not, in all likelihood, the model for most, if any of the Daniel(s) who are to be found in the canonical or deuterocanonical works of that name—we have become acquainted with in recent times through the Ugaritic texts as an ancient Canaanite figure noteworthy for his personal justice and for the efficacy of his sacrificial prayer.[2] And Job, of course, is a man of prayer and sacrifice who hails from the land of Uz.

We are persuaded that this geographical index should be taken seriously and not simply as a piece of theologizing indicating some never-never land of fancy.[3] True, the index is theological: Uz has a dimension that goes beyond the merely geographical. From the strictly geographical viewpoint, it might be considered to be a site in northern Syria (cf. Gen 10:23) or—as is more likely—in southern Edom (Gen 36:28). The latter is more likely because Job's "friends" are also Edomite Arabs: Eliphaz the Temanite (cf. Jer 49:7, etc.: *teman* often means simply "the southland"), Bildad the Shuite (Gen 25:2), and Zophar the Naamathite (cf. Josh 15:41)—all of these are southern sites on the march of Judah.

Edom is most likely, too, because Edom—along with Egypt—

was regarded as the source of Israel's "wisdom" (1 Kgs 5:10; Jer 49:7), of the philosophy and way of life in this world, including the arts (1 Kgs 5:11; Ethan, Heman, et al. are Arab "Ezrahites," i.e., aboriginals in Canaan, cf. Pss 88:1, 89:1).

This suspicion is only strengthened when we learn that Job was "perfect and upright . . . godfearing and eschewing evil." This is wisdom language (cf. Pss 25:21, 37:37; Prov 3:7, etc.). From the standpoint of the conventional wisdom, which was the wisdom of a this-worldly recompense that corresponded in exact proportion to this-worldly performance, Job was worthy of all blessings. So—even though they may have been misinterpreted and oversimplified—the prophets of Israel had taught. Prophetic teaching, as Job's friends were soon to demonstrate, could easily be bent to such a dogma. Meanwhile, while we are told that Job was indeed blest with the good that might be expected as the reward of wise and prudent living, he is also said to have been a model of ritual observance. There is irony here, undoubtedly, from the perspective of the author of Job— irony in correspondence with his parody of the wisdom tradition, in which a sectarian cultic life had no part to play. Recall, too, that Job is being portrayed as a prosperous Edomite sheikh who at the same time is practicing a levitical law one of whose prime purposes was to inculcate an orthopraxis by which precisely such as were God's true people would be distinguished from Edomite and other Gentiles.

"Maybe my sons have sinned and misspoken God in their hearts." The sin in question is what a later theology would classify as material rather than formal, that is to say, a word or deed which is wrong and immoral when considered objectively and in the abstract, but which has been committed inadvertently or under other circumstances which mitigate or remove entirely culpability. Only for such sins was there a provision for ritual expiation of the kind which Job is represented as performing (cf. Lev 4). Sin, in the Israelite mind, was a disturbance of right order which had to be rectified, regardless of the presence or lack of malice on the part of the sinner.[4] For conscious, deliberate, malicious sinning there was no ritual expiation (cf. Ps 51:18). That kind of sin could be forgiven and forgotten only through the extraordinary dispensation of a merciful God.

The sin in this instance is qualified as something by which Job's sons could have been considered to have "misspoken" God in their inmost thoughts ("their hearts"), possibly their subconscious, careless and unguarded thoughts. "Misspoken" is our paraphrase of a Hebrew verb that would literally have it that Job's sons had "blessed" God. Everyone recognizes that we are in the presence of a biblical euphemism or pious "correction" of the text. The biblical scribe, whether he was the original author of the text or a later copyist of it, could not bring himself to put down in cold writing an expression that was materially blasphemous, and therefore he preferred to write nonsense, which was at least pious nonsense. The same euphemism or alteration is to be found below in v 11 and in 2:5,9, and likewise in 1 Kgs 21:10, 13 and Ps 10:3. Its prevalence might indicate that it is a product of later scribal scrupulosity rather than of delicacy on the part of the original biblical authors.

The five verses above are a unity. They conspire in the presentation of a man who is completely righteous according to the norms by which contemporary Israel accounted righteousness. He is this despite, or in virtue of, his status as a privileged "patriarchal" character, like Abraham, Isaac, or Jacob of old—or like their compeers Lot, Ishmael, and Esau (father of the Edomites): representatives of the upright character inculcated by wisdom both in Israel and in the entire known world of the East.

> 6 *It happened one day as the sons of God came to present themselves before Yahweh, the Satan also came along with them.*
> 7 *Yahweh asked the Satan, "Whence do you come?" "I've been inspecting the earth," said the Satan to Yahweh in reply, "walk-*
> 8 *ing it up and down." "Have you remarked my servant Job?" Yahweh asked of the Satan. "Have you noticed that there is nobody on earth like him, a perfect and upright man, god-*
> 9 *fearing and eschewing evil?" The Satan answered Yahweh:*
> 10 *"Why shouldn't Job fear God? Haven't you put a hedge all around him and his household and all his possessions? You have blessed everything he has done and he is well-nigh worth*
> 11 *the earth. But just put out your hand, touch him in all he has, and let's see what he will throw in your face!" "All right,"*
> 12 *Yahweh said to the Satan, "whatever is his is at your disposal. Just don't touch him in his person." Immediately the Satan left Yahweh's presence.*

These verses also form a unity. The old folkstory begins in its presentation of the temptation of the patient Job.

Yahweh, the God of Israel, now appears on the scene, but in the guise of any god of the Gentiles (as Yahweh once may have been, ere Israel recognized his and its destiny, cf. Deut 32:8–14), that is, a chief god with subordinate deities ("the sons of God") within his heavenly court with whom he holds levée on stated occasions. On one of these stated occasions appears "the Satan." The word means "adversary" or "challenger." We are not yet at the stage of theological development when, under alien influences, biblical religion would posit a personal dualism of Evil *versus* Good, a Devil who would stand in counterpart to God. "The Satan" here is merely one of God's angels, perhaps a touch more skeptical than the rest of his angels, but in any case merely an *advocatus diaboli,* not the *diabolus* himself. All he wishes is to test the fidelity that the Lord has ascribed to Job.

And, to be sure, the Satan's challenge to God is fair enough. "I've been rich and I've been poor," goes the not too cynical line, "and believe me, it's better to be rich." Benevolence and good deeds come easy to the wealthy and well-positioned. The Satan knows very well—he seems to suggest that God does not know it equally well—that benevolence is a commodity hard come by in the poor, particularly in the poor that once knew better days. Thus the Satan is authorized, quite reasonably, to put to Job his first temptation.

Strangely enough, however, or—when we think of it—really not that strangely, we have nothing in the following verses about Job's being delivered over into the power of some alien force. What now happens to Job simply "happens": it is God's work. The Satan of this prologue is, in reality, nothing other than the left hand of God himself. What happens to Job is the work of the Lord, and the just cause of all his plaints.

> 13 It happened one day when his sons and daughters were eating
>   and drinking wine in the home of their eldest brother that a
> 14 messenger came to Job, saying, "Your oxen were ploughing
>   and the asses were pasturing alongside them when the Sa-
> 15 beans descended and stole them away. They also put all the

> *sons and daughters to the sword, and only I alone escaped to tell you."*
>
> *16 While he was still speaking another ran up to say: "Lightning fell from the sky and burnt up both the sheep and the sons and daughters who were shepherding them. It devoured them, and only I alone escaped to tell you."*
>
> *17 While he was still speaking another ran up to say: "The Chaldeans called up three bands; they made a raid on your camels and stole them away. They also put all the sons and daughters to the sword, and only I alone escaped to tell you."*
>
> *18 While he was still speaking another ran up to say: "Your sons and daughters were eating and drinking wine in the home of*
>
> *19 their eldest brother when a tornado blew out of the desert and levelled the four walls of the house. It fell on all the sons and daughters⁵ and they died, and only I alone escaped to tell you."*

Job's wealth melts away. Sabeans, lightning, Chaldeans, tornado—we might be tempted to think of natural predators alternating with acts of God, but in reality they are one. "Sabeans" and "Chaldeans," whatever their historical identity, were in the time of the author of Job roughly the equivalent of the "Huns" and "Vandals" of a later generation. They are ciphers only. By a frightful concatenation of events Job is stripped of all his possessions. His sons and daughters might be reckoned as ciphers, too, in this acceptation, for they figure here only as another mark of that state of former opulence of which Job is now bereft. Children, indeed numerous children, were counted as the most evident sign of the "successful" man, blessed by his God (see Pss 127:3–5, 128:3–4).

The narrative, as it unfolds, is characterized by stereotyped language and contrivances that contribute nothing to verisimilitude but are the obvious traits of popular storytelling.

The Satan has lost the first wager, it immediately appears. Job has been touched in "all that he has," but he is far from throwing anything in the face of God. Rather,

> *20 Job then tore his mantle, shaved his head, fell to the earth*
> *21 and prostrated himself, saying: "Naked I emerged from my*

> *mother's womb and naked I shall return there. Yahweh gave*
> *to me and now Yahweh has taken it back. May the name of*
> 22 *Yahweh be blessed." In no way during his distress did Job sin*
> *nor did he give cause for God to complain against him.*

This is indeed the proverbial patient Job. Tearing the clothes and shaving the head, not to mention other kinds of disfigurement (cf. Lev 19:28), were and are the signs of mourning for many different peoples. There was nothing reprehensible in Job's mourning his ill fortune. No one—least of all, perhaps, an Oriental whose routine gestures other men might think to be extravagance—is expected to greet with high good humor a turn of fate that has changed him from the darling into the plaything of the gods. It is his humble posture and his words of resignation accompanying the mourning rites that mark him the man of virtue. Here is the *insha'llah* ("if God wills") of the East.

It may be thought part of the Oriental exuberance that Job makes the seemingly impossible groveling protestation that he is prepared to return to his mother's womb as naked as the day he was born, should this be the Lord's will. However, in his commentary on the Book of Job Marvin Pope has correctly caught the sense of the verse[6] and has rightly related to it the words of Ben Sira (Sir 40:1):

> A great anxiety has God allotted,
>   and a heavy yoke, to the sons of men;
> From the day one leaves his mother's womb
>   to the day he returns to the mother of all the living.[7]

Job is talking about Mother Earth, of which we are all formed (cf. Ps 139:13, 15): dust we are, and unto dust we shall return.

> 2:1 *It happened again[8] one day as the sons of God came to pre-*
> *sent themselves before Yahweh, the Satan once more was in*
> 2 *their midst to present himself before Yahweh, and Yahweh*
> *said to the Satan: "Now whence do you come?" "Again I*
> *have been inspecting the earth," the Satan replied to Yahweh,*
> 3 *walking it up and down." "Perchance you have remarked my*

servant Job?" Yahweh asked of the Satan. "Perhaps you have noted there is nobody on earth like him, a perfect and upright man, godfearing and eschewing evil? He is still a model of
4 perfection. Truly, foolishly did you provoke me to try him." The Satan's reply to Yahweh was: "Skin for skin!⁹ Everything a man has he will give in place of his life. But now,
5 put out your hand again, touch him this time in his bone and flesh, and let's see what he will throw in your face!" "All
6 right," said Yahweh to the Satan, "he is yours. However,
7a keep him alive." So again the Satan left Yahweh's presence.

There is more than one bit of whimsy here. Besides the subtle modifications in the telling of a story that at first glance looks like a piece of *déjà vu,* there is some unspoken irony. The Satan, after all, has lost a bet. True, no wager was specified beyond the reputation of the bettors. At the very least, however, it appears that the Satan has lost face. Nothing is made of this, unless we are justified, as I think we are, in reading the Lord's words to the Satan in this second scene as crisply sardonic: the veiled sarcasm of one intelligent person speaking to another with the full expectation that his understatements will be appreciated and wincingly felt. Again it appears that Job has anticipated Goethe, or Goethe has penetrated Job, when we read in lines 350–4 of the Faust (Mephisto's soliloquy after leaving the presence of the Lord):

Von Zeit zu Zeit seh' ich den Alten gern,
Und hüte mich, mit ihm zu brechen.
Es ist gar hübsch von einem grossen Herrn,
So menschlich mit dem Teufel selbst zu sprechen,

which could be rendered,

From time to time I am in full accord
To look the Old Man up to have a chat;
It's most genteel of such a noble Lord
To take it from the Devil tit for tat.

At any rate, the Satan now acts with *huspâ,* impudence—and he
is heard! The Job who, when touched in everything that he possessed, was supposed to have thrown God's providence in his face,
rather has blessed God. So he will continue to do when touched "in
his person," the further and final persecution which the Satan wrests
from the Lord. Again—at least in the folkstory—the wager will be
lost and forgotten, and, for that matter, we hear no more of the Satan. He has served his narrative purpose.

> 7b Then he afflicted Job with a loathsome eruption from the tip
> 8 of his toes to the crown of his head. He picked up a potsherd
> to scrape himself with and took a seat on the refuse heap.

The "he" of v 7b is, of course, God himself: all of Job's afflictions come from him. It is pointless to inquire here what precisely
was Job's loathsome eruption, since it is quite evident that the point
of the story was to identify it as the very worst possible thing short of
death itself. Job's response is to pick at himself with a potsherd
(which he would have readily found on the refuse heap): was that to
alleviate his itching or to perform an act of penance? No matter; one
or the other is equally acceptable. The main point being made is that
he presents himself in a posture of penitence (cf. Jon 3:6). As in the
loss of his goods, so is Job in the affliction of his person: he is as quite
resigned to the divine will as he was in the preceding passage.

And now we come to uncertainties. The first verses involve
Job's wife and are as follows:

> 9 His wife then said to him: "Do you intend to remain this
> model of perfection forever? Speak a word to God and then
> 10 die!" He answered her: "Now you are talking like the fool
> woman you are. If we have accepted good from God,
> shouldn't we accept bad as well?" In no way during this dis-
> tress did Job speak a sinful word.

The original story may or may not have included Job's wife in
its cast of characters. Job did, of course, have a wife, or possibly several wives, in the manner of a great sheikh, to account for all those

children, both those whom he has now lost and the others who will be born after his restoration. However, this lady appears here so casually, only to disappear again so utterly, one may suspect that she is an afterthought in the story. Or rather, she is a redactional element (a stock character: the good man's harridan wife, his Xanthippe) introduced by the author of the canonical Book of Job in his adaptation of the old folkstory.

I am impressed by the argument of Hans-Peter Müller[10] that Job's wife is a new invention introduced into the story to assume the role of tempter formerly fulfilled by Job's friends—who now quite obviously have been accorded an entirely different function in the poetry of chaps. 3–31. In turn, as we shall see in a moment, it is likely that in the poetry the friends now perform—in intent if not in effect—the consolatory offices attributed to Job's relatives in 42:11, a verse that otherwise seems to be an irrelevancy in the present work.

As the text now stands, Job's wife does the Satan's work, exhorting Job to "throw into the Lord's face" all the evil that has been done to him. The "speak a word to God" of v 9 is, again, the euphemistic "bless God" that we have seen before.

The ancient Greek Septuagint translation of the Book of Job, perhaps to compensate for the small walk-on part that has been assigned to the wife in the canonical text, has provided her with the dialogue of a Greek tragic heroine, none of which has much to do with the surrounding context, either in the Hebrew or the Greek:

After much time, his wife said to him: "How long will you keep your peace, saying, 'Behold, I shall wait a bit longer, counting on the hope of my salvation'? For behold, your memory has already vanished from the earth, along with sons and daughters, the sorrows and pains of my womb which in vain I reared with hard labor. But you, you sit infested with worms and spend your nights outside, while I am a roamer and a toiler, wandering from place to place and from house to house, counting on the sun finally to go down that I might have rest from the toil and the sorrows that now encompass me. Just say a word against the Lord, and end it all."

The text is interesting, first of all because the Septuagint of Job tends to be an *epitome* rather than an integral translation of the Hebrew text, and therefore any *pluses* of the Greek over the Hebrew are interesting; and it is interesting because behind the Greek of this text which we have rendered fairly literally above, more than once a Semitic original seems to be peeping through—or, if not a Semitic original, then a good imitation of one. But we cannot pursue the subject here.[11]

> *11 When three of Job's friends heard about all this evil that had befallen him they came, each from his own place, Eliphaz the Temanite, Bildad the Shuite, and Zophar the Nahamathite. They agreed to come as a group to grieve with him and console*
> *12 him. But when they caught sight of him from afar they could hardly recognize him. They broke down in loud weeping and each one tore his mantle as they scattered sand over their*
> *13 heads to the sky. Then they sat down with him upon the ground for seven days and nights saying not a word to him, for they saw how terribly great was his grief.*

We should bring in at this point a verse that seems to be out of place in its present context but is remarkably parallel with the above passage. In chap. 42 of the canonical Book of Job, there is an easy transition from v 10 to v 12; v 11, on the other hand, seems to be an intrusion:

> *42:11 Then came to him all his brothers and sisters and prior acquaintances. They ate food with him in his house, consoled him, and comforted him over all the bad that Yahweh had brought upon him. Each of them also gave him a piece of money, and each of them a golden ring.*

It is easy to see both why 2:11–13 and 42:11 are parallel, and why 42:11 is uncomfortable in its present context. In both cases we have people coming to comfort Job—and, as far as the friends are concerned, definitely not with the intention of forming the inquisition *in re Job* that we find them conducting in chaps. 3–31 of our text. As for the relatives and acquaintances, what consolation and what comfort should they be expected to bring to one who has just been, in his latter days, blest above all other men? What do their "piece of money" and "golden ring" contribute to the latter days of Job as described in 42:11–16?

It seems likely that Job's friends were originally conceived as precisely that, consolers, condolorous with their brother Job, assuming the posture of the now dispensable "brothers and sisters and prior acquaintances" of 42:11. It is likely, too, that their original role was similar to that of Job's wife in the present tale, that in their commiseration with Job they tempted him to "misspeak the Lord"—the very thing, in fact, of which Job himself is most guilty throughout most of the poetry of the book! This supposition of the original bent of the folkstory provides the most natural accounting for what was once meant in 42:7–8, according to which the friends are condemned for having spoken ill of God in contrast to Job—the patient Job—who has spoken well. (We know, of course, that the eventual author of the Book of Job has made these words mean something quite else to agree with his poetry and his reconstitution of the friends' role.) Whatever evil the friends might have uttered against the Lord, we are reminded, might be, and in fact probably was in the mind of the author of the story, quite unwilling. Only such unwillful sins were patient of expiation rites.

The three friends, as we have seen, are all doubtless Edomite in origin, and all have good Semitic names. That they "agreed to come as a group" means that they had resolved beforehand to make their visitation a ceremonial occasion. Obviously they view Job, as the text says he is to be viewed, as a hopeless case, worthy of their pity but capable of no help they can offer. Casting the dust of the ground above or upon the head is a sign of hopelessness and frustration (cf. Josh 7:6; 1 Sam 4:12, etc.).

Now, we have taken the story almost to the dénouement, omitting the climax. The climax, of course, is quite different in the canonical Book of Job—which we shall try to explore below—from that which obtained in the original folkstory: the patient Job rewarded for his blind and unswerving fidelity. In the following verses of chap. 42 we bracket certain phrases not necessarily to indicate that they were not in the original story but rather to suggest that in the final poetic work they have acquired a new significance. And, for reasons noted above, we omit v 11.

> 7 [*And so, after Yahweh had spoken these words to Job,*] *Then Yahweh said to Eliphaz the Temanite: "My wrath is kindled against you and your two friends, for you have not spoken*
> 8 *seemly to me as has my servant Job. Now, then, get yourselves seven bulls and seven rams, and go to my servant Job. Offer up for yourselves a sacrifice and have my servant Job pray for you. I vow to accept his plea not to deal with you as your folly*
> 9 *deserves. For you have not spoken seemly to me as has my servant Job." Then Eliphaz the Temanite, Bildad the Shuite, and Zophar the Nahamathite did as Yahweh had commanded them, and accepted Job's plea.*
> 10 *Then Yahweh restored Job's fortune* [*after he had prayed for his friends*]. *Yahweh added to Job twofold everything that he had had before.*
> 12 *Then Yahweh made Job's latter days happier than the first. He had fourteen thousand sheep, six thousand camels, a thou-*
> 13 *sand yoke of oxen, and a thousand she-asses. He also had*
> 14 *seven sons and three daughters. The first he called by the name Paloma,*[12] *the second he named Cassia, and the third*
> 15 *Cosmetique. There were not to be found in the whole earth women as beautiful as Job's daughters.*
> 16 *He made them heiresses alongside their brothers. So afterwards Job lived for a hundred and forty years. He saw his children and his grandchildren, four generations.*
> 17 *Then Job died, an old man full of days.*

This is the classical ending to a patriarchal legend. Job's 140 years of life can hardly be anything else than a better than "ideal" span of years, like Abraham's 175 (Gen 25:7), Isaac's 180 (Gen 35:28), Jacob's 147 (Gen 47:28), and Joseph's 110 (Gen 40:26). All these other ages may have had numerical significance in themselves individually for the tellers of the Israelite folkstories. What they all evidently have in common is that they surpass by far the "ideal" three-score-and-ten of Ps 90:10—and in the case of Job, the number is surpassed precisely by one hundred percent.

And so, we are brought to the conclusion of a story which, originally, formed a part of conventional wisdom, even and including the Israelite adaptation of wisdom, which had incorporated into wisdom the piety of prophetical religion. The just are rewarded, the wicked are punished. The reward of the just is life, long life, "eternal" life, i.e., life that continues indefinitely in one's *zikrôn,* his memory and memorialization that are preserved by his children and in the repute he has gained in what he has done, what he has contributed. To have existed in the world without affecting it one way or the other, to have taken from it and to have given it nothing, is not to have lived. For such as these, therefore, there is no life beyond. To those who have lived meaningfully, there is indeed life, and the measure in which they have contributed to the meaning of all life is the measure of their own eternal life.

Sometime in the same era in which the Book of Job was being composed—when the folkstory that we have been considering was being worked into the poetic work at which we shall soon be looking—the tragedian Sophocles was ending his *Oedipus Rex* with his Greek chorus dolefully affirming that no man shall be accounted happy till he has run the mortal race and there is no further chance of catastrophe. The Greek Oedipus has sometimes been compared with Job, and certainly there is some basis for comparison—in the poetry of Job, perhaps, more than in the prose, simply because in the poetry the hiddenness of purpose of the Hebrew God can appear quite as capricious as the *anangkē,* necessity, fate, which the gods of Olympus decree as Oedipus' destiny, their never explained intent to toy with him and destroy him; the prose of Job, of course, has rationalized the "demonic" quality of the divine (precisely as has 1 Chr 21:1 revising 2 Sam 24:1) by introducing a third person, the Satan, into the encounter, superficially resolving this character by transforming it into a reluctant (and carefully hedged) transitory "temptation." (In a rather different fashion, a rather different thing has been made of the story of Abraham's "temptation" in Genesis 22, which a perhaps more perceptive Jewish tradition has termed "the binding of

Isaac.") The demonic quality of God (cf. Exod 7:3–4; Isa 6:9–13, etc.) will occupy our attention greatly as we try to perceive the message of Job in the following pages.

Prose and poetry, however, join as one with Sophocles in their description of what was to be counted as happiness in the human estate. To have lived well was to have died in tranquillity, "full of years." To have lived very well was to have seen not only one's children but also the children of those children, the guarantee of immortality. "I have been young, and now I am old," stoutly protested the psalmist of Ps 37:25, "yet never have I seen the righteous forsaken, nor his children begging bread." Is this a true asseveration born of experience, or is it the stout protestation of a true believer for whom contrary evidence needs not even be investigated? No matter, it is the doctrine of the prose of Job, which is bitterly assailed by its poetry without, however, another doctrine to oppose it.

How much the prose and poetry together of Job were later to clash with a new orthodoxy is indicated by the Septuagint addition to the final v 17 of the last chapter of this book. We have translated that v 17 "Then Job died, an old man full of days," adhering to the letter of the text. Marvin Pope has made a felicitous paraphrase: Job was "old and satisfied with life." For obviously that is the sense: having seen his children and grandchildren to four generations, Job's immortality was ensured and he could not hope—no one could hope—for anything further. Yet the Septuagint adds: "It is written, however, that he will rise again with those whom the Lord raises up." The new orthodoxy undoubtedly felt this line to be a necessary codicil to an otherwise inconsequent and perplexing barrage of words and counterwords. Both the folkstory and the Job *diatribē,* on the other hand, doubtless would have regarded this pat "solution" as a pathetic travesty of the Job problem.

There are some further Septuagintal additions which leave us in no doubt as to their provenance and derivation. Some of the manuscripts read:

> This Job is explained in the Syriac Bible[13] as living in the
> land of those who inhabit Aulis [Uz, for these purposes], on
> the borders of Idumea [Edom] and Arabia;[14] formerly his
> name was Jobab [for this name, and those of Zerah and

Bozrah below, see Gen 36:33]. Having taken an Arabian woman to wife he sired a son whose name was Ennon [the Anub of 1 Chr 4:8?], but he himself was son of his father Zare [Zerah], one of the sons of Esau, and of his mother Bosorra [Bozrah], so that he was the fifth from Abraham. Now these were the kings who reigned in Edom, over which land he also ruled: first Balak the son of Beor [actually, according to the scriptural evidence, Balak was the son of Zippor (Num 22:2)], by whose name his city was called Dinhabah [1 Chr 1:43]. After him was Jobab also called Job, and then Asom [could correspond with various Semitic names, e.g., Hûhšām (cf. 1 Chr 1:45–46)], the governor from the country of Teman; and after him Adad the son of Barad who destroyed Midian in the plain of Moab, the name of whose city was Gethaim [the names are ancient, the combinations later]. The friends who came to him were Eliphaz, of the sons of Esau the Themanites, a king; Bildad the ruler of the Saucheans; and Zophar the king of the Minoans.

Though the passage may be historically worthless, still the associations have a definite literary interest.

Notes

1. So Hermann Gunkel, *Genesis* (Göttingen: Vandenhoeck & Ruprecht, 1964) 66; Gerhard von Rad, *Genesis* (The Old Testament Library; Philadelphia: Westminster, 1961) 126. In the mind of other recent commentators, gratitude or thanksgiving for deliverance is the leitmotiv of Noah's sacrifice; cf. Benno Jacob, *Das Erste Buch der Tora Genesis* (New York: Ktav [1974]) 227; Robert Davidson, *Genesis 1–11* (The Cambridge Bible Commentary; Cambridge University Press, 1973) 86; Claus Westermann, *Genesis* (BKAT I/8; Neukirchen-Vluyn: Neukirchener Verlag, 1973) 607.

2. Cf. G. C. L. Gibson, *Canaanite Myths and Legends* (Edinburgh: T. & T. Clark, 1978) 103–122 *passim*.

3. So Manfred Görg, "Ijob aus dem Lande 'Uṣ': Ein Beitrag zur 'theologischen Georgraphie,' " *Biblische Notizen* 12 (1980) 7–12.

4. Cf. Bruce Vawter, C. M., "Missing the Mark: The Biblical Theology of Sin," *The Way* 1 (1962) 19–27.

5. Here, as in vv 15, 16, and 17, "all the sons and daughters" translates the Hebrew *nĕ'ārîm*, lit. "young people." Evidently the storyteller intended by this repeated phrase to anticipate the climax achieved here when the "young people" are indeed Job's "sons and daughters."

6. *Job* (AB 15; Garden City: Doubleday, 1965) 16.

7. According to the *New American Bible*.

8. This narrative reiterates the language of 1:6–12 with occasional significant variation which I interpret to be the insinuation of irony. I have tried to reproduce this by varying the translation accordingly.

9. The Satan is obviously quoting a popular proverb to the Lord. Both evidently understood it, as we do not precisely. The general sense is, apparently, that a man will forgo all that he has to avoid personal injury.

10. *Hiob und seine Freunde: Traditionsgeschichtliches zum Verständnis des Hiobbuches* (Theologische Studien 103; Zürich: EVZ-Verlag, 1970).

11. The Septuagintal translation of the Book of Job is a fascinating subject in itself, which has been thoroughly, if only partially, explored by Homer Heater, Jr., in his *A Septuagint Translation Technique in the Book of Job* (CBQMS 11; Washington: Catholic Biblical Association, 1981). On pp. 31–36 Heater discusses this speech by Job's wife as a prime example of anthological (or, as he terms it, anaphoric) composition from other biblical passages, mainly those of the Book of Job itself.

12. Paloma, Cassia, Cosmetique: The Hebrew had Jemimah ("dove"), Keziah ("cinnamon"), and Keren-Happuch ("container of kohl," i.e., the powdered antimony used as mascara). The names are obviously intended to be "exotic" and "genteel." The pretentious pseudo-names I have invented try to capture the spirit of the originals.

13. The Syriac Bible, viz. the Old Testament as read in the early Syrian church. The standard version is called the *Peshitta*, i.e., "vulgate." Whether this version, into the Eastern Aramaic dialect known as Syriac, is of Jewish or Christian origin cannot be determined on the present evidence. Cf. A. Vööbus, "Bible, IV," *New Catholic Encyclopedia* 2, 434. The Septuagint itself, of course, though of Jewish origin, has also been transmitted to us almost exclusively through the hands of Christian scribes.

14. "Arabia" at this time encompassed all the land (and lands) south of Damascus and east of the Jordan River.

4.

IN SEARCH OF THE REAL JOB

In the previous chapter we have seen the story of Job, a figure of ancient folklore, devoted and unquestioning servant of God whose closeness to the Deity constituted him a proverbial intercessor to atone for the shortcomings of lesser men. What we are now about to see is a very different person, the protagonist of the poetry of Job 3:1–42:6 alike to that of the prose story hardly in anything other than name, though it is clear enough that the poetry has been spun from the prose as a presupposed. While the prose story is complete in itself or, in the form we now have it, nearly so, the poetry requires the prose for its *mise en scène.* There are those who believe that the author of the poetry also composed the prose story to serve as his introduction and conclusion—that is, that he had no ready-made folk story but composed his own from old recollection of the Job name. For reasons that I hope are persuasive, which in any case I have indicated in the preceding pages, I believe that the prose story not only preexisted the author of the poetry of Job but that it had passed through various stages of development before it was adapted by him—somewhat less than perfectly—to adjust to the rather alien designs that he held for the Job figure.

In any event, it is the poetic Job and the poetic Job alone who is of interest to the sensitive observer of religious experience. As John L. McKenzie has properly remarked of the prose story:

An edifying story it suffers from the common plague of edifying stories, which is that it is so unrealistic that it be-

43

comes revolting. It is not faithful to life and it is not faithful to God. We do not believe that God plays games with human life. Only people do that. Had it not been for the Israelite poet, that sickly story would no doubt have sunk into deserved oblivion. But the poet caught the hero, who does not know what is going on, at the very bottom of his misfortunes and imagines how he might ask why everything happens to him. That celebrated question has never been so well asked.[1]

The judgment is perhaps a trifle harsh against the prose story. While it may be true enough that the poet of the Job dialogues has parodied the conventional wisdom purveyed by the prose Job, still he selected for the purpose a sturdy vessel worthy of his improving mettle, not a barrel in which to shoot fish. Untrue to life it was, but not, unfortunately, untrue to what is perceived as life by probably the majority of our fellow beings. The author of the poetry of Job did not achieve literary immortality by tearing down a childish fable but by building on a theme that needed restatement.

Neither, of course, is it a question of comparing prose with poetry, as though one were the better of the other or the prior of the other. We all remember the story of the autodidact who was delighted to learn that all his life long he had been speaking prose. Aside from the fact that it is probably impossible to make a clean distinction between prose and poetry in general, or biblical prose and poetry in particular,[2] that apparently naïve reaction might not have been so far from the mark after all. "Prose" has about it the sense of speech that is "straightforward" (*prorsus*); and anyone who has tried to write it carefully knows that the path straightforward is never obvious but has to be discovered and contrived, often painfully. It is not prose but rather poetry—at least in its more obvious manifestations or devices of rhyme or cadence or meter or high-flown idiom—that becomes the medium of expression of the common man. Witness the jingles of TV, of Muhammad Ali, or of country music. As an earlier Richard Burton once observed, "The Arabic is a language in which, like Italian, it is almost impossible not to rhyme."[3] And that is not wholly untrue of other tongues.

The author of the dialogues of Job did not create his masterpiece by despising, either in its message or in its medium, the folk-story on which he built. He created it, as we have suggested above, first of all by a recasting of characters, so that the persona of the one and only protagonist, the true Job, might appear unembarrassed by the simplism with which popular lore had surrounded him. The method that he followed is not hard to discern, for in its own way it was rather mechanical and quite predictable. The friends of Job, his comforters of 2:11–13 (and 42:11, probably), do not relinquish their well-meant, kindly function; they simply become irrelevant comforters in view of the more refined vision of the ways of God which had been revealed to the poetic author.[4] Because of his vision, all the characters in the Job drama have taken on new dimensions.

It is not hard to see how, in general, the author of the poetry of Job outlined his work.[5] He began, after the prose prologue, by introducing Job, the real Job, in chap. 3 with his celebrated plaint: Better were it had I never been born! In reply, each of Job's friends responds each three times, to each of which responses Job counterreplies. This takes us to chap. 28 where there is an excursus on the inaccessibility of wisdom, then to chaps. 29–31 where Job makes a final summation, and then to chaps. 32–37 where there is an intervention of the young man Elihu, and finally to 38:1–42:6, the dialogue between God and Job preceding the prose epilogue.

First of all, we have to acknowledge that the poet's intentions have not been carried out quite as he planned them. The Book of Job, which is not very much understood today, was hardly understood in its inception and certainly was not by some of those who transmitted it to us, and as a result the text has become mixed up, added to, and confused in any number of ways.

Job's plaint certainly occupied chap. 3. His friend Eliphaz makes his first intervention in chaps. 4–5, and Job replies to him in chaps. 6–7. The second friend, Bildad, is heard in chap. 8, and again Job replies in chaps. 9–10. The third friend, Zophar, appears in chap. 11, to be answered by Job in chaps. 12–14. So far so good; it is even possible to find a distinctive poetic beat in the lines attributed to Bildad on the one hand and Eliphaz on the other, and in the respective responses of Job, as well as other artistic devices.[6]

The second series of discourses, while not quite as satisfactory as the first, also seems to follow without undue difficulty. Eliphaz

speaks again in chap. 15; Job replies in chaps 16–17; Bildad is heard
again in chap. 18; Job responds in chap. 19; then Zophar in chap. 20;
and Job answers Zophar in chap. 21.[7]

It is in the third series of discourses that we sense that something is seriously awry in the received text. It begins fairly enough:
the speech of Eliphaz in chap. 22, perhaps with a bit of transposition
of verses, including part of chap. 21 taken from Job (cf. the order of
verses in the *New American Bible*), reads not unreasonably. But Job's
answer in chaps. 23–24 is, at least in its entirety and as it stands, in-
coherent with the thought of the protagonist. Bildad may have had
his final word—an uncharacteristically brief one—in chap. 25. But
then comes chap. 26, most of which hardly looks like the speech of
Job, though it is ascribed to him, and then chap. 27, of which the
same judgment must be made. Doubtless in these chapters, misunderstood, abbreviated, and misconstrued by subsequent tradents, are
at least the vestiges of Job's answer to Bildad, Zophar's final statement, and Job's response thereto, the reconstruction of which is subject to considerable conjecture.[8]

Once the poet had completed his somewhat ponderously struc-
tured series of dialogues through which he had set forth the *prob-
lema* of the tortured Job and of those—the poet himself,
particularly—who spoke through him,[9] he brought his work to its
conclusion—it would be premature, perhaps, to call it a solution—in
chaps. 29–31 and 38:1–42:6. These passages represent Job's final, re-
iterative protestation in spite of all the words of "consolation" he
had heard from his compeers. He still demands his answer and, it
appears, he receives it, such as it is, and acquiesces in it, such as it is,
in a series of passages that rings true with what we would expect
from this author.[10]

We shall consider separately these passages as they relate to the
plaint of Job and his canonical spokesman. It remains to consider in
this preview chap. 28, the paean to wisdom, and chaps. 32–37, the
intervention of the young man Elihu.

As far as chap. 28 is concerned, probably no one will demur in
the judgment that it has been intruded into the text without regard to
its literary context.[11] At the same time, no one will also deny that it
has been appositely added, by someone who rightly caught the mind
of the author of Job and wished to sum up his propositions in a cap-

sular form.[12] Or, that is to say, caught the mind of the author of Job in his principal affirmation, which was to deny the efficacy of wisdom as a solution to man's problems because of the simple and very evident fact that wisdom completely eludes man's grasp. We say that this was evident because it was evident to the author of Job and to those who empathized with him: quite evidently it was not evident, indeed it was anathema, to the wisdom tradition within which the author of Job wrote and discovered his heretical identity. We shall have to take a closer look at Job 28 later on.

About the Elihu speeches an altogether different judgment must be made. They were composed not by someone who understood Job but by one to whom the book was a puzzlement and perhaps a scandal, who thought that the conventional wisdom expressed by Job's friends had not been fairly and evenly dealt with, and who, therefore, in his unimaginative way concluded that the balance could be redressed by the addition of another half dozen long-winded chapters of sermonizing. The chapters have their own fascination: in 32:1 it is made plain that their author recognized that Job thus far had had the best of the argument and that something further must be said. His mistake, however, was to conclude that the argument needed further carrying on and that it had not been rendered totally moot by the ensuing pronouncements of the Lord. The Elihu speeches are presented as the exasperated expostulations of the neo-orthodox who wants to see defended redoubts which his ancestors in the faith have finally abandoned as hopeless. The chapters are certainly pertinent, therefore, to the overall purpose of the Book of Job, but they also stand as a wry memorial to its failure to have achieved understanding before ever it was accepted as a canonical book. The speeches are a pastiche of threadbare arguments already discarded, seemingly to be refurbished only in the repetition,[13] a fact of which the ancient Greek translator of the Hebrew Bible seems to have been well aware and on which he improved.[14]

In such ways, therefore, and by refusing a journey into convenient byways, did the author of Job pose the question of the real Job. It will be our task now to see how successfully he accomplished this search. It is a search in which we are still all engaged—all of us, that is, who hold to the quixotic view that the world should make some sense, and that if faith must supply where sense fails, at least it should not be expected to blot sense out. The man of faith does not ask that the world be totally intelligible, that wholly unattainable goal of the irremediable romanticist; he only asks that it be moderately so. That was and is the purpose of the quest of "wisdom."

Leo Rosten[15] has recited a delightful little anecdote which suits our purpose at this moment:

On the eve of Yom Kippur, the most solemn and sacred day, an old Jew looked up to heaven and sighed: "Dear God, listen: I, Herschel the tailor, put it to You! The butcher in our village, Shepsel, is a good man, an honorable man, who never cheats anyone and always gives full weight, and never turns away the needy; yet Shepsel himself is so poor that he and his wife sometimes go without meat! . . . Or take Fishel, our shoemaker, a model of piety and kindness—yet his beloved mother is dying in terrible pain. . . . And Reb Label, our *melamed* (teacher), who loves all the lads he teaches and is loved by all who know him—lives hand to mouth, hasn't a decent suit to his name, and just developed an eye disease that may leave him blind! . . . So, on this most holy night, I ask You directly, God: Is this *fair?* I repeat: *Is this fair? . . .* So, tomorrow, O Lord, on our sacred Yom Kippur—if You forgive us, we will forgive You!"

This passage has more than one function. It demonstrates, among other things, that the questioning of Job has never really been answered, neither by Hokhmah nor by the Synagogue nor by the Shtetl, neither by the Church nor by philosophy nor by theology, nor by whatever takes their place in these modern times.

I say this not to discourage us in our quest, but merely to make us wary.

Notes

1. *How Relevant Is the Bible* (Chicago: Thomas More, 1981) 96.
2. Cf. James L. Kugel, *The Idea of Biblical Poetry. Parallelism and Its History* (New Haven: Yale University Press, 1981).

3. Cited in J. M. Rodwell, *The Koran* (London: J. M. Dent & Sons, 1950) 18.

4. Cf. Walter Vogels, P.B., "Job a parlé correctement," *Nouvelle Revue Théologique* 102 (1980) 835–52.

5. In what follows I am using, more or less, the analyses made by Patrick W. Skehan, beginning with "The Book of Job," in *Studies in Israelite Poetry and Wisdom* (CBQMS 1; Washington: Catholic Biblical Association, 1971) 78–82.

6. See, in detail, Skehan, "Strophic Patterns in the Book of Job," *Studies* 96–113, here especially the structure outlined on p. 99.

7. *Ibid.,* 108–110.

8. *Ibid.,* 110–113.

9. In *The Structure of the Book of Job* (Philadelphia: Westminster, 1981 [a translation of the author's *Der Aufbau des Buches Hiob* of 1977]), Claus Westermann has consistently maintained that the Book of Job is not a "problem" book but rather a lament, during which interchange the friends of Job proceed in their consoling role from attempted persuasion to disputation and finally to accusation. For Westermann, however, both Job's and the friends' theologies have to be corrected and replaced in the Book's final dénouement. Problems there are, therefore, whether or not they are explicitly asserted by the biblical author.

10. Cf. Skehan, "Job's Final Plea (Job 29–31) and the Lord's Reply (Job 38–41)," *Studies* 114–123.

11. Cf. Pope, *Job* xviii.

12. So Franz Hesse, *Hiob* (Zürcher Kommentar AT 14; Zürich: Theologischer Verlag, 1978) 158; Eduard Nielsen, "Homo faber—sapientia dei," *Svensk Exgetisk Årsbok* 41/42 (1976/77) 157–65.

13. Cf. David Noel Freedman, "The Elihu Speeches in the Book of Job," *Harvard Theological Review* 61 (1968) 51–59.

14. Cf. Heater, *A Septuagint Translation Technique* 97.

15. A wise man who, like all wise men, is not always wise, who sometimes expects the baker to have sliced the *challa.* The citation is from *The Joys of Yiddish* (Penguin Books, 1971) 4.

5.

JOB VERSUS GOD

The author of Job is in a quarrel with God. How do you engage God in a quarrel? With what God do you quarrel? Many names of God occur in the Book of Job. First of all, it appears that only in the prose prologue and epilogue, and in the divine monologue/dialogue of 38:1–42:6 built on the prose story, is the name Yahweh, the specific name of the God of Israel's covenant and religion, featured. The only exception to this rather inflexible rule takes place in Job 12:9, where in the received Hebrew text the name Yahweh does appear, but where we also have good textual reason to suspect that the original reading was a more neutral term for "God." This incidence is doubtless not without its theological significance: the traditional God of Israel who, in the ancient story, had tested Job and proved him true, now, in these more sophisticated times, has to respond to him and give an accounting of his serene authority. It is the kind of response to which less authorities in our days have been called upon to account for their stewardship and have failed the test entirely, substituting for the *de facto* simply the fiction of *de iure.*

Is there a further key to the message of Job in the other terms that have been employed to represent the Deity? In the term Shaddai, for example, one of the most ancient terms by which the God of Israel was acknowledged by his devotees? This has been asserted, as though the Shaddai ("the Almighty") of Job 5:17, etc., etc., represents only a partial revelation of divinity, something that could be figured by a later piety in terms of guardian angels or "the Lady Wisdom," or the like.[1] It is more probable that the divine surrogates of

El, Elohim, Eloah (the last possibly an artificial back-formation), and so forth, are deliberate archaisms designed to lend an "authentic" color to the discourses of Job. (It may be of note that the Elyon-["the Most High"] title of God, known to us from the Pentateuch and from the Psalms, where it must have played a large role in the Jerusalem liturgy, never occurs in Job.) And thus, it is far more probable that divine traits are far more significant in Job than are divine names.

Divine traits. To what God is Job implicitly pleading in his initial complaint, when he cries:

> Damn the day when I was born
>   the night when they said: "It is a boy!"
> Let that day count as darkness,
>   let not God (*Eloah*) above recall it,
>   nor light shine upon it.

Though this may sound a bit blasphemous at first, something at least very novel in Israelite piety, it is not that at all. One of the laments of the prophet Jeremiah (from which, as a matter of fact, the Job poet may have taken his inspiration) reads much the same:

> Cursed be the day
>   Whereon I was born!
> The day my mother bore me,
>   Be it ever unblessed!
> Cursed be the man who brought
>   The news to my father,
> "It's a boy! You've got a son!"
>   (Ah, how glad it made him!)
> Let him be, that man, like the cities
>   Which Yahweh overthrew without pity!
> Let him hear a shriek in the morning,
>   The shout of battle at noon!
> Because he killed me not in the womb;
>   So had been my mother my grave,
>   And pregnant forever her womb.

> Ah, why came I forth from the womb
>   To see but trouble and grief,
>   And end my days in shame? (Jer 20:14–18).[2]

This complaint, be it noted, was lodged against the providence of Yahweh, the God of Israel, in the heyday of Israel's Yahwistic piety by one of Israel's most certified prophets. And it was accompanied (Jer 20:7) by a truly audacious claim of *force majeure:* "You seduced me, Yahweh!" (the same verb for seduction in Exod 22:15 and Judg 16:5: Delilah over Samson!). "I let you seduce me. You overpowered me and you triumphed." The almost coarse overtones of the passage resist any mitigation of translation. In all the rest of Job 3 there is nothing to compare with this earlier, savage plaidoyer against Yahweh by one of his devout followers.[3]

Thus far, therefore, the poetic Job stands in the posture in which Claus Westermann wants to leave him, the classic posture of the complainer before God, content if only his wailings be heard by whatever supernal powers hear such pleas beyond God. Probably Job remains in this posture throughout much of the Jobian poetry, probably even in the famous verse of Job 19:25:

> I know that my *gōʾēl* lives,
>   my second will stand upon this soil.

For, despite the resonances of "I know that my Redeemer liveth"— and without any intention of denigrating the glories of Handel's oratorio, the product of a vastly different construction of the biblical texts—it appears that in this verse appeal is made not to the God of Job's complaint but rather to a heavenly (i.e., non-earthly) witness (cf. Job 16:19), who can serve as his vindicator, testify in his behalf[4] before that supreme court of fitness and rightness to which both God and man are subject. In Job's understanding, his vindicator may have been simply Job himself, or the merits of his case which is Job existentially, his life and his fate making up that witness which in Jewish law is also the case for the prosecution.[5]

If it is true, however, that Job begins, and to a large extent continues, as a straightforward lament, it is also true that the book soon begins to probe more deeply into the relation between God and man.

The occasion of this probing is provided to Job by the inept consolations of his friends.

In the first round of talks, Eliphaz sets the tone. Job, he insinuates, is hoist on his own petard, a wise man who is now denying to himself the counsel that he has formerly offered so freely to others (Job 4:2–6). Think upon that ancient counsel, Eliphaz says: "What innocent person perishes? Since when are the upright destroyed?" (vv 7–11). This is, on the one hand, prophetic religion: the conviction that weal and woe are dispensed by the Almighty in correspondence with a people's fidelity or infidelity to its covenant commitments. It is also a travesty of prophetic religion when that religion was transmuted by wisdom into a way of life for the average man. Eliphaz admits this incongruity and cloaks it discreetly within the guise of a special revelation—hardly a revelation to the wisdom community—that no man may consider himself to be righteous simply by his willing it so and so striving for it (vv 12–21).

If there is contradiction here, it is intentional, part of the message of the Book of Job. We should not expect—a fatal flaw in some of the interpretation that has been given the Book of Job—that the lines assigned to Job's friends and consolers are universally intended to add up to a consistent argument. In chap. 5 Eliphaz acknowledges (vv 3–7) that the righteous do not always presently prosper nor do the unrighteous always presently decline (Psalm 37), but at the same time he is utterly complacent about the ultimate correlation of personal righteousness with the good life. Neither will Job's protestation of innocence permit any evidence to be brought forward to shake this inflexible rule: the built-in safeguard to the logic of Eliphaz is its inconsistency, the escape clause in which he claims in the same breath that before God no one can be righteous. Furthermore, if even the angels are not without fault (4:18), it is senseless to think that they (the "holy ones" of 5:1) could serve as intercessors for Job. He adds, somewhat sententiously (v 8):

> In your place, I would appeal to God (*El*),
> and to God (*Elohim*) I would state my plea.

Insofar as Job has not invoked any angelic assistance and has, implicitly at least, already been pleading with God, a plea which becomes quite explicit in his following responses, it is not immediately evident what precise import Eliphaz intended his words to have. Possibly he means that while Job has been complaining—senselessly—about God, he should instead be pleading with him for understanding, an understanding which Eliphaz's philosophy commits him to believe is entirely possible.

In 5:17 he insinuates another argument, that afflictions from God are somehow medicinal, meant for the betterment of the temporary sufferer, who will eventually prosper. The argument is not much developed, and probably for this reason a later editor of Job, to whom the argument evidently meant much and who thought it had not been given proper weight in the discussions, in chap. 33 reassigned it to the intrusive figure of Elihu. Eliphaz, for his part, evidently feels little need of it, for the traditional wisdom he has thus far expounded requires no further justification. In 5:27 he brings his remarks to an abrupt close with the peremptory injunction that Job cease his foolish talk and bow to the age-old doctrine that he should know as well as any other.

If Eliphaz had hoped quickly to bring Job to submission, he obviously failed signally. In the first place, Job continues his lament, in terms every bit as bitter and presumptuous as before (6:1–12 and 7:1–10). Then he turns on his friends, reproaching them, as represented in the windy discourse of Eliphaz, for their worse than uselessness, their betrayal of their function as advisers to the perplexed (6:13–30). What are friends for, if not to console, to support, to strengthen in need? Yet he, who had hoped for such a service, is rather in the position of one of those thirsty caravans in the desert which stake their all on finding a water source at one of its uncertain wadies, turn aside in this hope, and perish when they are greeted by a dry arroyo. Only at the end (7:12–21) does Job respond to Eliphaz's advice to appeal to God, but then in a fashion hardly to do other than outrage Eliphaz and to make him view it as a personal affront.

Job's word to God might, at first glance, almost seem to be the one to which his wife in the prose Prologue had urged him (2:9). It is typical of the brash and impudent Job of the poetry, at any rate. Almost contemptuously, he avoids the use of any of those traditional divine names with which the Book of Job is otherwise filled. Rather, he speaks to the "man watcher" (v 20) in a parody of the concept of a God of providence. "What is man that you should be mindful of him?" asked the psalmist of Ps 8:5, marveling at the attention the Deity has lavished on its creature man. Job also marvels, but sarcastically, at attention which is so unwelcome and malign. Is he, an insignificant man, the Sea or the great Dragon of the sea, here called Tannin but elsewhere Rahab or Leviathan (cf. 9:13, 26:12, 40:25–26; Ps 65:8, etc.), those primordial forces which the God of the heavens had to contend with and vanquish in a display of divine power (v 12)?[6] Even if Job had sinned, in what way could it have hurt God (v 20)? In short, God is a bully, harassing one who is powerless to defend himself. The language of Job is bumptious, even a little coarse. Commentators usually note that in v 19 there is an idiom in use till today among the Arabs: "Give me time to swallow my spit"—we might say: "Let me catch my breath." Enough already, Job is saying; leave me alone for a while. Soon he will be dead in any case, and then it will be too late for God to think better of his conduct and have mercy (v 21).

Job's impudence doubtless explains the testiness of Bildad, who now breaks his silence in chap. 8. He is much more callous than Eliphaz in dealing with Job's situation, for he is a true believer to whom persons are less important than principle. He, too, is the complete traditionalist to whom a new outlook or a possibility of some exception to the rules is unthinkable. He consequently contributes no new thought to the presentation of the case against Job. In these verses, as already in some preceding and to follow, it is evident that the author of the poetry of the Book of Job is aware of the prose story into which he has integrated his work. It also looks as though the author is having a bit of fun with Bildad in the process. In v 5 Bildad thinks to satirize Job's impertinence of 7:21 about God's seeking him out by insisting, rather, that it is Job's obligation to seek God out (the same Hebrew verb is used in both verses). But in v 20, when he confidently affirms that God will not cast away the upright (*tam:* the word used of Job by Yahweh in 1:8, etc.), he ironically forecasts the judgment of 42:8 in a way that his narrowmindedness could never have encompassed.

Job's reply in chap. 9 is less to Bildad the platitudinarian than it

is to the propositions enunciated by Eliphaz. At the same time it is a
far more radical reply than he had made before, and perhaps we are
expected to attribute its recklessness to the intransigence of Bildad.

First of all, says Job, it is self-evident to him that no one can be
justified before God (so Eliphaz in 4:17). It is self-evident, however,
not only because of his admitted omnipotence evidenced in the creation and maintenance of the universe—an awesome power which
Job can only reverence—but also because the omnipotence and om-
niscience of God are the arbitrary exercise of a supernal power in the
face of which man is both powerless and helpless. This is Job's flat
rejection of the traditional wisdom. Wisdom decreed that God punishes the wicked and rewards the just, and that in doing so he exer-
cises eminent justice. But who is to say that God is just if the only
measure of this justice is what God does? There is no impartial arbi-
ter to determine this case (v 33). Job—man—is entirely at God's
mercy on his own recognizance, with no appeal. In vv 28–31 Job
seems to address God himself to this same effect, again without nam-
ing him. Contrary to the conventional wisdom, the empirical evidence on which his friends thought that they could rely testifies not
to a rational moral order in the universe but rather to its opposite (vv
22–24; cf. Eccl 9:2–3):

> It is all one! therefore I say:
>   Both the innocent and the wicked he destroys.
> When the scourge slays suddenly,
>   he laughs at the despair of the innocent.
> The earth is given into the hands of the wicked;
>   he covers the faces of its judges.
> If it is not he, who then is it?

In chap. 10 this God (*Eloah*) is addressed himself, in much the
same terms in which he has been spoken about in chap. 9. It is the
Eloah of Job's experience, not of his friends'. And while the address
is direct, yet it is still kept at one remove. Job cries out (to the reader,
to the proverbial disinterested hearer, to whomever) that such and
such he *will* protest to this God (v 2). It is as though he cannot bring

himself even now, perhaps especially now in view of the verses quoted above, to speak face to face and existentially with this God who has made himself so remote, alien, and inaccessible.

Zophar, the third of Job's friends, now utters his speech (chap. 11), least imaginative of the three and, mercifully, the shortest, though it also serves to provoke the longest of Job's replies thus far. If Zophar contributes anything at all, it is the thought that the wisdom which Job professes to despise is equally unassailable with the God whom Job professes to reject, since it is God's very gift to man, that which has been provided by which man may truly know the true God. This is the doctrine of Proverbs 1–9 and other wisdom writings; it is not, of course, the doctrine of the Book of Job.

Job's answer is long, but it also has an air of finality . As for wisdom: He knows its ins and outs as well as do his friends, and he also knows its shortcomings which they will not acknowledge (12:1–13:2). As for God: It is Job and not his friends who speaks rightly about Shaddai and El (13:3–16), a contention that will be validated by Yahweh in the dénouement of 42:7. Not Job but rather his friends have falsified the image of God by trying to bend it to their preconceived ideas of what God must be. In v 16 he even ventures the wistful thought—which is quite possibly confirmed in the Epilogue of the Book of Job—that he will be proved righteous and not impious in the very fact that he has presumed to speak honestly about God. And finally, as to God: In 13:17–14:22, probably all the way through, Job addresses God, as usual without any invocation by name. Essentially, he says nothing to God in these verses that he has not said about him in the foregoing.

The *dramatis personae,* the elements of the drama, and the entire burden of the argument have now been disclosed. Two positions stand in total contrast. For Job God is a being totally powerful and by that same token totally free of every constraint, including the constraint of human grasp and reason, a God, therefore, to whom he cannot even put a conventional theological name if he would try to call upon him. This God is totally free, with a freedom of action that does not correspond with man's thoughts of what is the responsible use of freedom or with his concepts of what is right and just and proper. On the contrary, for Job's friends God is their own reason and righteousness writ large. The two positions are clear-cut and obvious.[7]

Is it necessary to puruse these dialogues further in order to penetrate the riches of the Book of Job? In one sense, certainly yes, for in the chapters that follow there is some of the best of Hebrew poetry that is part of man's best literary heritage. From the standpoint of the development of theological argument, however, we have already heard just about every detail that the author intended to explore. The rest is artistry. The "consolers'" diatribes become harsher, more unfeeling, even irresponsible, shrill and petulant, in even proportion with Job's increasing intransigence and weary spurning of all their best efforts. Let it suffice for us simply to highlight just a few of the more significant verses.

In chap. 15 Eliphaz professes to be scandalized at Job's refusal to bow to the current wisdom and begins an *ad hominem* personal attack on Job's integrity that anticipates the truly unforgivable charge that he will lodge in chap. 22. Job, in turn, in chaps. 16–17 makes no effort to hide his disgust at the tedium to which he is being exposed by these empty words. He continues his lament, to which he feels he has full right, and in 16:18–19 he issues another almost blasphemous challenge to which he implicitly dares God to respond:

> O earth, cover not my blood,
> nor let my outcry have a resting place.

This is an obvious reference to Gen 4:10. Words flung into the teeth of the God (Yahweh) who first pronounced them: Innocent blood—the wanton and casual slaying of a just man—utters a cry for vengeance that cannot be stilled. But what if, as now appears, the one who slays or who is about to slay is God himself, this God of hoary tradition? In such a case, Job can only appeal to a God beyond God:

> Even now, behold, my witness is in heaven,
> and he who speaks for me is on high.

There is, Job wants to believe, an answer to the riddle of his life, and the life of everyman, than whatever has been dreamt of in the philosophy of his friends.

Bildad's second speech and Job's reply in chaps. 18–19 add little to the story or to the development of its protagonist. However, it might be noted that elsewhere the poetic author has assimilated skillfully into his composition the prose prologue and epilogue on which he built; the assimilation has not been carried out with high art in 19:13–19, which only with difficulty are reconciled with the rest of the story. We shall also pass over without comment Zophar's second speech (chap. 20) and Job's sixth reply (chap. 21).

We will not venture any further commentary on the discourses, chiefly because of the impossibility of reconstructing what the original sequence of the passages was, before editors, some understanding and some misunderstanding, began to work on the materials of this book. The sole exception we shall make is for chap. 22, which we can confidently accept as Eliphaz's final effort, at the same time his confession of the total bankruptcy of the wisdom argument that he and his fellows had tried to adduce against Job. In the event, it will prove that only to this final argument will Job deign to make a counter-appeal, in the chapters that follow. It will be an easy counter-appeal, because the final thrust of Eliphaz is the cheapest of all shots. Eliphaz has lost so far every argument against Job; therefore he now resorts to abuse, accusing Job in meticulous detail of the most specific violations of social and ethical imperatives (see especially vv 6–11). In Eliphaz's simplistic mind the logic of this unfair, unjust, totally unconscionable accusation was perfect and flawless. God visits no miseries except on sinners, and since Job's miseries are immense, therefore so must have been his sins. The rest is mere deduction, requiring no proof, no evidence, and certainly not the intrusion of reasonable doubt. Eliphaz is defending a principle and, like many other pious people before and after him, he defends it at all costs and with a casual disregard of fairness and the right of persons to their good name.

Job's answer to this irresponsible charge actually occurs only in chap. 31, as part of his final summation of his case before the response of Yahweh that comes from the whirlwind (chaps. 38–41). We will see Job's final plea again later on in connection with Yahweh's reply, but it is appropriate at the moment to cite a few verses from it (31:13–15) which should have a peculiar interest for us. It is a fairly well-known citation. Job says,

Had I refused justice to my slave or slave-girl
    when they had a case against me,
What then could I do should God [*El*] rise against me,
    what reply to him should he demand an answer?
Did not he who made me in the belly make him also?
    Did not the same one fashion us in the womb?

The words are important because we have to put the ethical standards of the Book of Job in proper chronological perspective. Another century and more would elapse before the Greek ethicists, from whom we in the West, with the mediation of Rome, inherit much of our ethical theory and imperatives. There is, it may be asserted, nothing in Aristotle or Seneca or Marcus Aurelius that approaches this vision of the oneness of the human species, regardless of whatever distinctions circumstance may have decreed. (For Aristotle, in his *Nicomachean Ethics,* a slave was an *organon empsychon,* an "animated instrument.") And this is not to bring into contrast the hopelessly perverse and blasphemous titles under which professedly "Christian" countries in even later times blessed the peculiar institution of human slavery not merely in terms of the *status* that had been bestowed it in Roman law but also in virtue of their determining the slave to be outside the human race, without rights, without innate dignity.

    Eliphaz and Job, in other words, are at one as to what adds up to good moral conduct. We shall see more of this in the following chapter. The quarrel of Eliphaz and Job is not over morality but theodicy.

    Job and his friends have, at least for our purposes, concluded their dialogue. For the most part Job has professed his bewilderment at the travails visited upon him; he has overtly questioned whether the God of Israel's traditional titles would respond to him and therefore—irresolutely?—has refused to call upon him by any of these titles, though he has obviously been speaking to God. What we now have to see is his final plea and the reply of the Lord, which is supposed to be the end and conclusion of the Book of Job.

Notes

1. So Bernhard Lang in *Der einzige Gott. Die Geburt des biblischen Monotheismus* (Munich: Kösel-Verlag, 1981).

2. Translation of John Bright, *Jeremiah* (AB 21; Garden City: Doubleday, 1965) 130.

3. In "Anders als er wollte: Jer 20, 7–13," *Bibel und Liturgie* 54 (1981) 179–188, Franz D. Hubmann insists on the one hand that the prophet's lament refers to past experiences and also that in these verses he identifies himself with the people Israel. In any case, however, the language of Jer 20:7 remains unprecedented.

4. On the concept of the *gō'ēl*, see my article, "Salvation Is a Family Affair," in *Sin, Salvation and the Spirit* (Collegeville: Liturgical Press, 1979) 65–70.

5. Cf. Évode Beaucamp, "Le goël de Jb 19, 25," *Laval Théologique et Philosophique* 33 (1977) 309–10.

6. This is a motif of Canaanite mythology appropriated rather often in the poetry of the Old Testament and used as a conventional symbol of Yahweh's supremacy.

7. Cf. Frederic Raurell, "Ètica de Job i llibertat de Déu," *Revista Catalana de Teologia* 4 (1979) 5–24.

6.

WHAT DOES GOD WANT?

As we have seen, Eliphaz and Job are entirely at one in making the service of the fellow the measure of the service of God, in equating social morality with the righteousness by which a person may account himself righteous in the sight of the Lord. Not with an absolute righteousness, of course: both have agreed that no man can make any such claim. But, on the other hand, with some sort of claim by which without vain pride or self-deceit an honorable man may rightfully distinguish and separate himself from the ungodly. That "we are all sinners together" is inescapably a true axiom of the human condition; it becomes true, however, only when uttered by one who has eaten of the tree of the knowledge of good and evil and knows the difference between the two, preferably, therefore, by a saint. It is a meaningless and pernicious platitude when it is proposed as an objective standard of human behavior: if St. Francis of Assisi and Adolf Hitler are both sinners who have been born into a sinful race and have themselves sinned, what in the world do we put down as the common denominator of "sin"?

Within these realistic qualifications, Job declares himself to be a just man and Eliphaz, without evidence and with the rashest of possible judgments, declares him to be the opposite. And the two have the same criteria by which this relative justice is determined. And both share the conventional wisdom, that God rewards the just and punishes the wicked. Hence Job's problem and perplexity, and hence Eliphaz's callous and *a priori* rashness.

The origin of this doctrine, we have already stated, is rooted in the teaching of the great prophets of Israel and is, in part, also a distortion of that teaching. It is also, however, a doctrine of Israelite "wisdom," a doctrine which in Israel grew up alongside the prophetic tradition, was influenced by it and influenced it in a uniquely Israelite symbiosis. Both in the time of prophetic activity[1] and later—in the time of the Book of Job—when prophecy had ceased to be an effective voice in Israel and wisdom had moved into the vacuum which prophecy had created by its passing, the wisdom tradition enjoyed a long history of commonsense practical morality based on a common human consent as to what was right and proper and which, therefore, should be acceptable to the appropriate cultural Deity.

Israel never made any bones about the fact that it had inherited most of its culture from outside: from Canaan, much of its mythology, much of its ritual; from Mesopotamia, much of its mythology, its calendar, many of its ritual practices; from Egypt, its wisdom ideals and many, many words and other ideas; from Edom—whence comes the Job story—many other ideas along with a plethora of Arab tribes who were "naturalized" into Israel by way of convenient genealogies provided by the Chronicler and others.

The wisdom tradition of basic morality associated with the service of God is variously traced in the Bible to Egypt (1 Kgs 5:10), to Edom (Jer 49:7), to the Phoenicians (1 Kgs 7:14), to the "Chaldeans" (Daniel 1:20)—in short, it was recognized to be an international and non-sectarian phenomenon. Those who were in Israel accounted "the wise"—in whose fellowship Job is obviously to be counted as an heretical member—we would probably characterize today as "intellectuals," "thinkers," "one-worlders," people who found more congenial the company of skeptics, inquirers, and questioners in the great wide world outside to that which was available at home in the comfortable confines of family, tribal, and national hearth. They were, in their day, today's ecumenists and world federalists.

We can single out for special mention in this connection the wisdom of Egypt only because it is the best documented for this period.[2] The wisdom fraternity—as we can judge from this literature—dealt with a single deified figure in its confrontations with Deity. There is no question of a theoretical monotheism: only one god—nemesis—could be coped with at any single time. We may remember that in the poetic Book of Job God is never named by its protagonist direct-

ly in any address to the Deity, though the traditional names of the
God of Israel and of Israel's antecedents wander in and out of the
poetry. In Egyptian wisdom—which might, by its own etymologies,
be characterized as "life-lore"—*maat,* sometimes but not necessarily
deified, is the equivalent of the Old Testament language of *ṣedeq* or
mišpāṭ, "justice," "order," "righteousness," "what is proper," "what
is right," "what ought to be done." We can also add to these considerations the fact that the Egyptian "wisdom" literature that precedes
the Israelite was largely a literature of protest against the insensitiv-
ity of the gods, and that is the essence of Job's plea.

Morality is, as the term might indicate, the *mores* or customs of
a given people, society, tribe, class, or nation: whatever is considered
to be right and proper. Quite obviously, it is not an easy task to make
an objective judgment as to what is *the* morality in any particular situation. What is moral is what the common consent of mankind—
without which moral judgments would be irrelevant—has judged to
be a proper and rightful subject of ethical inquiry.

In Egypt the connection between religion and social morality
was certainly not unknown. In the *Protests of the Eloquent Peasant,* a
wisdom writing of the Middle Kingdom,[3] the Peasant of the story appeals to the Chief Steward as "the father of the orphan, husband of
the widow, brother of the divorcée, the apron of him that is mother-
less," insisting that "doing justice is the (very) breath of the nose"
(= the Hebrew *rûaḥ,* essentially the same as *nĕšāmâ* or *nefeš,* the
very principle of life itself[4]). It is significant, perhaps, that the text of
Job employs this concept of *rûaḥ* preeminently only in the Elihu
speeches (33:4–5, 34:14–15, 37:9), possibly inspired by the Eliphaz
usage (4:15) on which they are modeled; in any case, this is wisdom
language that not only is ordinarily eschewed by the prose and poetry of Job but is also often ridiculed by it (in 1:19, 7:7, 8:2, etc., *rûaḥ*
is simply "wind" or "idle wind").

The Peasant continues by exhorting the Steward to "do justice
(*maat*) for the sake of the Lord of Justice, of whose justice true justice exists." It is hard to avoid the conclusion that in the wisdom of
Egypt no less than in the wisdom of, say, Proverbs 1–9 in the Israelite tradition—and from a much more venerable age[5]—there was presupposed a notion of divine justice according to which men's actions

were to be measured and their degree of righteousness in God's sight calculated accordingly.

The ideal king, which is to say, in more native Israelite language, the judge, i.e., the one who makes justice prevail, is likewise a wisdom concept which Israel shared with or had borrowed from its elder neighbors. So ideal, in fact, is the regal justice portrayed in such passages as Psalm 45 or Isa 11:1–5, for example, that a later piety would hardly credit it to be capable of a fleshly human being, but must be reinterpreted to apply to a future, not-this-earthly dispensation—in Jewish expectation, the apocalyptic world-to-come, in Christian thought the "spiritual" fulfillment in the new Israel. However, nearly a millennium and a half before the coming of the Christian era, a myth from northern Canaan could represent an upstart heir and would-be usurper rebuking his aging kingly father in these terms:

> Hear, I beseech you, o noble Keret,
> hearken and let (your) ear be attentive.
> While bandits raid you turn (your) back;
> and you entertain feuding rivals.
> You have been brought down by your failing power.
> You do not judge the cause of the widow,
> you do not try the case of the importunate.
> You do not banish the extortioners of the poor,
> you do not feed the orphan before your face
> (nor) the widow behind your back.
> Because you have become brother to a bed of sickness,
> companion to a bed of plague,
> come down from the (throne of your) kingdom (that) I may
>   be king,
> from (the seat of) your dominion (that) even I may sit (on it).[6]

We are invited to compare such biblical passages as Amos 5:11 and Isa 10:2 from the prophetical writings, and from the material vaguely characterized as "wisdom" Ps 82:2–4, Job 22:7–9 and 31:16–17, and Sir 33:13–14.

It is significant that in Israelite tradition what was elsewhere predicated of the king was here recognized to be a prerogative of everyman. That is true of the creation story of Genesis according to which mankind is created in God's image and likeness: strictly royal language in the context of Near Eastern divine kingship. It is true of the patriarchal legends, in which Abraham, Isaac, and Jacob are given divine imperatives as from a royal oracle and accorded the promises of progeny and dominion which were conventional kingly prerogatives. It is true of such Israelite literature as Proverbs, Ecclesiastes, even the Wisdom of Solomon, composed in Greek at a rather late date, which preserve the fiction that their aphorisms are, though obviously addressed to everyone, really the instruction that was customarily given to princes by court sages—Aristotle's tutoring of Alexander the Great or Macchiavelli's *Il Principe* are other examples of the genre—or, in turn, pronouncements of that wisdom-instructed king himself. For what the fiction preserves was, whether actually in Israel or only as a borrowed memory, an original face. It can also be plausibly argued that the correspondence between wisdom and prophetic language which we have already remarked more than once, the agreement on the social ideal, may have its prior explanation in the wisdom tradition which was accepted by prophecy.[7] Both prophecy and wisdom were introduced into Israel from without, and both were transformed by it.

That little detail of transformation must on no account be forgotten. In times past when the comparative literatures of Israel's contemporary neighbors were unknown, it was to be expected that the values communicated through the Hebrew Bible would have been thought of as the unique contribution to the human spirit made by ancient Israel. When the comparative literatures and histories were revealed through modern study, it was likewise to be expected, and certainly it occurred, that various enthusiasts proposed what have come to be called pan-Egyptianism, pan-Babylonianism, and, more recently, pan-Canaanitism, as the real origin of all that is most distinctly biblical religion. Such propositions could be more readily made in view of the fact that Israel's society, materially speaking, was in every one of these cases inferior to that of the alleged ideological source: Israel was always the borrower, not the innovator. Subsequent to and concomitant with these enthusiasms, there has been a tendency to try to retrieve biblical originality by denigrating the supposed parallels in law, ethics, religious and moral values. None of these expedients is necessary. Certainly it is not necessary to minimize the contributions that have been made to man's better thinking in ancient or modern times in order to defend what we might consider to be an even better thinking. Philo of Alexandria, who tried to persuade the Greeks that Moses had anticipated the thought of their philosophers, and the Fathers of the Church who treasured up the documents of the religions of antiquity (they are our only source for some of these treasures) which they classified as *Praeparatio evangelica* (Prelude to the Gospel), were far more enlightened than *conquistadores* who tried (and, predictably, gloriously failed) to install a new culture through the effacement of the old, or more recent amateurs who have confused biblical religion and bourgeois folkways.

We must, in any case, recognize the element of transformation. One of the most enthusiastic of all the Egyptologists was able to say, despite the citations we have made and the evidence we have given of Egypt's priority in social thinking, particularly in the Middle Kingdom period, that beyond these are to be found, in any case, "the same old hodge-podge of ritual, hymns, prayers, and magic spells" in the relics of this age.[8] There is no question that, quantitatively at least, the preoccupation of both prophecy and wisdom in Israel with the moral question radically differed from that which occurred in the religions of Egypt, Mesopotamia, and Canaan. So much so that documents which are analogically denominated "The Babylonian Job," "The Sumerian Job," "The Egyptian Job," and the like, are, not dissimilarly with "The Babylonian Genesis," in actuality vastly different kinds of compositions, connected superficially (synchronically) by any number of common themes and constants of the human mind, but separated substantially (diachronically) by all the history and experience that had gone into the making up of the separate conceptions. The quantitative, in other words, demands a qualitative explanation, which only history can supply. It may be said that we do not know the whole history and that therefore we cannot properly evaluate Babylonian, Egyptian, and Canaanite society in relation to the Israelite. I personally believe that this is not true, that it is a subterfuge equal to that which pious biblicists relied upon a couple of generations ago when they rebelled against the insufficiency (and the incorrect interpretation) of the secular documents that were being proposed as a challenge to biblical originality.

Today Egyptology is a venerable science, needing no credentials. It is very doubtful that anything essential is going to be added in our generation to the lore that we have acquired from this study. We know, without contest, that Israel's wisdom probably came from Egypt, and that Egypt was probably very formative in the beginnings of Israel as a nation and as a polity. Canaanite influence was always obvious: from whom else than from the indigenous population should a new society derive its rites, its architecture, its contact with the soil? It should certainly be no new revelation that the pottery and the buildings on one side of the Jordan as well as on the other—Moab and Israel—should have been indistinguishable in the days of "the Israelite conquest."[9] As for Mesopotamia, there is no need to document the route of dependence: Israel was always the recipient.

But then again we come to the question of that which accounted for this quantitative/qualitative aspect of Israelite tradition that distinguishes it from the traditions of admittedly superior and admittedly donor cultures to which Israel was beholden. Since we are not about to make a point of all this anyway, but have brought it up only to dismiss it from our subject matter, we have no hesitation with the suggestion that there was something about the religion of Israel among its contemporaries, some dynamism that they did not possess, that accounts for the different and successful use that it made of common principles. There is no way of demonstrating this hypothesis. It is a matter of prejudice, perhaps. If someone prefers to think that it is entirely by chance and the luck of the draw that the Hebrew Bible (together with and through its offspring, the Greek New Testament) formed what we are pleased to call Western civilization rather than the *Enuma elish* of Mesopotamia, the Keret Legend of Canaan, the *Instruction* of Amenemope of Egypt, or untold forgotten masterpieces of these and other kindred peoples, he is certainly free to do so. But it is fair to ask who, in such an instance, is the more credulous. These works, known today to a handful of the human race, and that only because an even smaller handful has taken the trouble to dig them from the sands and extract from their long forgotten scribblings some contact with the human spirits that once labored over them, are so known to us only because of that biblically formed Western civilization:

> Not that your gods are nine or ten,
> But because it is only Christian men
>   Guard even heathen things.

If, given the assumption, the Lawcode of Hammurabi rather than the Law of Moses had come down to us—apart from later archeology—as the legal heritage from the ancient Near East, would we now be seeking for remote parallels in the Law of Holiness or the Covenant Code? If we were the religious and cultural heirs of the Ugaritic myths or, later on, the *Corpus Hermeticum,* would we be testing out Hebraic thought patterns and cognate terminology gleaned from scraps that might be pretentiously titled when gathered together a *Biblia Hebraica?* If this appeals to some of our contemporaries as a realistic scenario, let them act it out. I prefer, however, to heed Hamlet's injunction that the drama o'erstep not the modesty of nature.

Why I am willing to let all this go, however, is that I think it totally irrelevant to the Book of Job. Certainly Job and his friends are in complete agreement that God's dispensation is to be measured according to the standard of *maat* or *ṣedeq,* that he is a just God rewarding the good and punishing the evil. All of them, too, Edomites though they were in the literary inception, are professing a doctrine which was, in the adaptation of the Job story in the form in which we have it, entirely Israelite, the product through centuries of prophetic and wisdom thought of a rational concept of God and of what is demanded by a moral God. It is a unique concept of God, not to be minimized in its time, not to be cheapened by pretended parallels, and not to be denied its relevance to our own times, when such a God may be thought most desirable to our needs.

The only discordant note is that such a God is not the one revealed in the final pages of the Book of Job.

Notes

1. Cf. the famous line in Jer 18:18: *torah* (instruction) from the priest, *ʿēṣâ* (counsel) from the wise, *dabar* (messages, words) from the prophets: the tripartite means of ascertaining the mind of God.

2. In this paragraph I am paraphrasing the findings of Michael V. Fox, "Two Decades of Research in Egyptian Wisdom Literature," *Zeitschrift für Ägyptische Sprache und Altertumskunde* 107 (1980) 120–135.

3. The 12th–13th dynasties of Egypt, ca. 2000–1800 B.C., a period of feudalism dominated by the chief families of Egypt, when a concept of bourgeois family values was dominant. For the *Protests,* see J. Pritchard, *Ancient Near Eastern Texts* 407–410.

4. Cf. Paul van Imschott, "L'esprit de Jahvé, source de vie, dans l'Ancien Testament," *Revue biblique* 44 (1935) 481–501.

5. It is generally conceded that Proverbs 1–9 has been constructed as a prologue to the rest of the book, whether that rest is thought to be of identical composition or of remote collection from the past. In any case, Proverbs 1–9 is among the latest material of this book, probably coeval with the Book of Job. Cf. Skehan, "The Seven Columns of Wisdom's House in Proverbs 1–9," *Studies* 9–14; "A Single Editor for the Whole Book of Proverbs," pp. 15–26; "Wisdom's House," pp. 27–45; and most recently, Otto Plöger, *Sprüche Salomos (Proverbia)* (BKAT XVII/1; Neukirchen-Vluyn: Neukirchener Verlag, 1981).

6. J. C. L. Gibson, *Canaanite Myths and Legends* (Edinburgh: T. & T. Clark, 1978) 102. The translation is of a part of the *Krt* myth in text 16 vi 42–54.

7. See William McKane, *Prophets and Wise Men* (Studies in Biblical Theology, 44; Naperville: Allenson, 1965).

8. John A. Wilson, *The Burden of Egypt. An Interpretation of Ancient Egyptian Culture* (University of Chicago Press, 1951) 118.

9. J. Maxwell Miller, "Renewed Interest in Ancient Moab," *Perspectives in Religious Studies* 8 (1981) 219–229.

7.

WHAT CAN WISDOM TELL US?

Before the dénouement—if it can be called that—of the Book of Job as it is now constituted, three literary complexes make their appearance.

There is, for one thing, Job's final peroration in chaps. 29–31. It is a peroration that adds nothing to what has gone before, for in what has gone before Job has accepted the premises of his friends with regard to wisdom's vision of the justice of God. He has demurred, and continues to demur, only in this respect, that in the one specific case of which he had full knowledge—his own—the vision has failed.

He recalls the idyllic days of his past when he was revered as one of the most successful and happiest of men, bearing a mien quite like that of the Job of the prologue (cf. 29:1–11.18–25). This condition was owed him, says Job,

> For I relieved the poor who cried out,
> and the orphan, those who had none to help them;
> I was blest by those who else would have perished,
> and I made the heart of the widow leap with joy.
> I donned righteousness and it clothed me,
> justice to me was like a robe and a cap.
> I was eyes to the blind,
> and feet was I to the lame.
> A father was I to the poor,
> and I pursued the cause of even those I did not know.
> I broke the jaws of the wicked,
> and forced their teeth to drop their prey (vv 12–17).

Job is, in other words, that parfait model of piety which should be, and had the right to be, the object of divine beneficence. Indeed, says Job,

> What is the allotment of God (*Eloah*) from above,
>   the inheritance of the Almighty (*Shaddai*) from on high,
> If not disaster for the wicked
>   and woe for the doers of evil?
> Let God weigh me, then, in the scales of justice
>   that he may acknowledge my innocence (31:3–4, 6).

Thus throughout most of the rest of chap. 31 he continues with protestations in the same vein, cataloguing all the good that he has done and the evil he has avoided consistently.[1]

And so, Job ends as he began, a complainer, in chap. 30 rebuking his friends for their lack of fellow-feeling and, in the process (vv 20–23), apostrophizing the God whom he refuses to name to be accountable to him on the terms of *ṣedeq* and *maat* which wise men had determined was the working of God. And in 31:35–37 he rests his case, on the same premises of his accusers and would-be comforters:

> O that I had an impartial judge,
>   here I sign: let Shaddai answer me!
>   Would that I had an indictment written by my adversary!
> I would wear it on my shoulder
>   and bear it like a crown.
> I would give him an account of all my steps,
>   like a prince I would approach him.

To the end Job shares with his friends the wisdom notion of God and his justice. The only difference between them is that Job knows himself to be a righteous man to whom much is owed by the God of wisdom, who has strangely and unjustly perjured himself by abdicating his traditional responsibilities toward his faithful clients. Job's friends have tried to retain the exact correspondence of human justice = divine justice—that is, the exact correspondence of wisdom with the nature of God—by making Job to be something less than an exemplar of wisdom's justice—though they acknowledge that so he had been—or by some other subterfuges. Job, without really knowing better, can only maintain his integrity by recognizing the error of his friends, an error not only in fact but also in principle.

There is also, in these chapters preceding the word of the Lord that begins in chap. 38, the speech of Elihu which occupies chaps. 32–37 in the existing Book of Job. As we have intimated earlier on, we regard these chaps. 32–37 to be an intrusion into the text on the part of some editor who, however well intentioned, misconstrued the ultimate message of the Book of Job and thought that by means of this interpolation he could better capsulate all the good arguments that had been raised against the obdurate Job, which he had apparently rebutted in the foregoing discourses. Elihu, as a matter of fact, contributes no new thought that has not already been exposed as threadbare. He is represented as a neo-conservative, a younger true believer whom a later editor thought should be given his head in a perhaps misguided conception of equal time allotted to dissentient opinion, however ill-informed and unprepared by any experience.

> Then the anger of Elihu, the son of Barachiel, of the family of Ram, flared up against Job, because Job held himself to be righteous rather than God (*Elohim*). And against his three friends his anger also flared up because they had not found a reasonable answer to reply to Job. Elihu had waited while they spoke because they were years older than he, but when he saw that the three had no further answer, his anger flared up.

And, therefore, he begins to speak, interminably. No answer is given by Job to Elihu's speech, a good sign that it didn't belong there in the first place. The speech itself is a *tour de force,* wholly forgettable in the context of the complete book. Elihu has nothing to say that was not said better by his predecessors, and the fact that he does not know this is testimony both to the callowness of the portrait that appears in these chapters and, possibly, to the artistry of the editor who introduced the figure into these chapters.

There is, finally, in these interstitial chapters, a notion of wisdom presented that is totally disconsonant with the concept not only of Job and his friends but also with most of the other literature that is called "wisdom" in the Old Testament—that is, the inaccessibility of wisdom, a thought that is proposed to us quite baldly in chap. 28.

Wisdom—that is, the ability of the human mind to work out through observation a satisfactory rationale of human life and mores in this world, to relate man to his fellows and the rest of the universe, and even (or especially) "to justify the ways of God to men"—probably achieves its ultimate apotheosis, as far as the Hebrew Bible is concerned, in the eighth chapter of the Book of Proverbs. Here, in a probably fairly late literary composition (Proverbs 1–9) that was designed to introduce the collections of traditional aphorisms and instruction that account for chaps. 10–31 of Proverbs,[2] the author personifies wisdom, not quite but almost as the Egyptians had divinized Maat, and makes of it the key to the meaning of man's world. Wisdom was, he says, a preexistent prior to God's creation, which the Lord took and made the principle of his creative acts, so that all that is and the why of all that is must be accountable to wisdom, explicated by wisdom.

> Mine is counsel, mine is sound advice,
>   I am insight, mine is strength.
> By me kings reign
>   and rulers decree what is just.
> By me princes rule,
>   and all the leaders who govern the earth.
> Those who love me I love in turn,
>   and those who seek me find me.
> With me are riches and honor,
>   enduring wealth and prosperity.
> My fruit is better than gold, even fine gold,
>   and my yield is better than choice silver.
> I walk in the way of righteousness,
>   along the paths of justice,
> Granting wealth to those who love me,
>   and filling up their treasuries (vv 14–21).

Thus speaks wisdom, and her meaning is clear. She, wisdom, is the inspiration and measure of all that is right in the world. To find her is to discover the way of righteousness. And this righteousness, the righteousness which walks hand in hand with wisdom, that self-same righteousness of which Job and his wise friends confidently assured themselves, brings with it—must bring with it—success, well-being, prosperity.

But there is more, far more. Wisdom concludes her autobiographical description in vv 22–31 with claims as audacious as they are breathtaking.[3]

> Yahweh took me to be the principle of his ways
> > before any of his primeval deeds.
> Before then, from of old I had been poured forth,
> > from the first, before the beginning of the world.
> When as yet there were no deeps I was brought forth,
> > while there were no springs burgeoning with water.
> Before the mountains were shaped,
> > before the hills, I was brought forth,
> When he had not yet made the earth and the fields,
> > nor the first clods of the soil.
> When he established the heavens, there I was,
> > when he traced a vault over the face of the deep,
> When he made firm the skies above,
> > when he made mighty the fountains of the deep,
> When he set limits to the sea,
> > lest the waters should o'erstep his command,
> > when he laid the strong foundations of the earth,
> There I was with him as a fellow craftsman,
> > a daily delight for him,
> > frolicking before him all the while,
> Rejoicing in the inhabitable world,
> > and delighting in the human race.

What is the claim of wisdom here, if it is not that it was a principle coeval with the creator God, a principle, a rationale, which enjoyed its existence independently of any determination by this God? This is not as much a revolutionary concept in human speculation as it might first appear. Many other thinkers who have contributed to our intellectual ancestry have thought of "natural law"—the area of

wisdom speculation—as constituting such a closed and inexorable
system that even God himself, its author, was only following out the
built-in rules of his own nature when he established and proclaimed
it. In reality, of course, "natural law" is only what it has been given
to the human mind to perceive as a rationale in the world that sur-
rounds it. But that is not the view of Prov 8:22–31, for which this
rationale was an already given at the beginning of time, which the
creator God could only accept and utilize more or less as a blueprint
in the elaboration of his creative design.[4] Certainly there can be no
doubt, for anyone who reads the verses above without preconcep-
tions, that wisdom asserts to herself an existence prior to that of the
created world (vv 24–29 rather obviously evoke the creation myths
of Genesis 1–3 and other similar passages), and that Yahweh is figured as having made use of wisdom in constructing the things that
are in man's world.

The corollary and pragmatic conclusion from such a construction is, of course, that by wisdom man may penetrate the mysteries
of his world and understand his relation to God the creator, since
wisdom has been God's companion in creation and since wisdom is
benign and totally accessible to the human race in which it delights
as the medium of God's creation. The rest of the Book of Proverbs is
filled with this conceit: by taking thought a person may account himself righteous in God's eyes ("the fear of the Lord is the principle of
wisdom"). It is the conceit of the very late book called the Wisdom
of Solomon, the Book of Wisdom *par excellence,* a Greek work composed in the Jewish diaspora probably about 100 years B.C., which
was (for obvious reasons) never accepted into the canon of the Hebrew Old Testament but which became a part of the early Christian
canon of the Old Testament for equally obvious reasons, namely that
it preserved in meticulous detail the age-old wisdom doctrine that
Job was written to combat. It is, finally, the conceit of the Book of
Sirach, this time an originally Hebrew work which also never
achieved canonical status (except, it might appear, by the Qumran
sectaries) for other reasons (its proto-Sadduceanism?), which not
only celebrates wisdom and personifies it as the principle of all creation, but also identifies it with the Law of God revealed in his Torah
(chap. 24).

All of this, an otherwise quite respectable strain of Israelite thought, is alien to chap. 28 of Job. This chapter has been variously described as "extraneous" to the Book of Job[5] and as "un-Israelite."[6] It is both of these things. It is extraneous, to the extent that it is hard to fit this passage—and not alone this passage, be it noted—into the structure, originally no doubt fairly rigid, which the author of Job's poetry first designed as his literary vehicle. Certainly it has no place as part of Job's argumentation prior to his "conversion." The best guess is that chap. 28 is a subsequent addition to the Book of Job, but an addition, in this case (in distinction to the Elihu additions), of an author who understood what the Book of Job was all about and decided to reinforce it with his own contribution. It is un-Israelite surely, but at the same time surely no less un-Israelite than the Books of Ruth, of Ecclesiastes, of Job itself, of the Song of Songs, of Ezekiel, all of which worked their perilous way into the canon *per aspera ad astra,* while other no less worthy efforts of late Israelite thought were doomed to perish utterly or to come down to us only fragmentarily or in exotic translations—Sirach, Enoch, Wisdom, Baruch, Judith, Maccabees, Tobit, etc. Alien? Only if it be thought that there was some kind of standard Judaism against which aberrations of this kind could be measured. But there was no such, not yet, not even in the time of Ezra and Nehemiah, not even in the sanctuary of the Palestinian Judaism of restoration, the province of Yehud (Persian, and then Hellenistic), let alone in the diaspora of foreign lands where more Jews were destined to dwell, as they have continually dwelt ever since, than have inhabited or who are ever to inhabit the land of Abraham's promise.

Failing prophecy, which had now all but disappeared from the Israelite scene, there remained wisdom, the instruction of the wise. Who could dismiss this accumulated wisdom, this tradition of the centuries, this common consent of Israelite and non-Israelite humanity which had agreed on the body of moral and social norms which experience had proved were both workable and practical? A close parallel is to be found in the beginnings of Christianity, when the earliest Christians, once they had recognized that their first notion of the imminent passing away of the world about them had been a premature vision, reconciled themselves to a continuing world that would have to be lived in by the conventional rules. Eph 4:25–32 affords a good example, where a typical taxonomy of Stoic virtues is held up for the emulation of Christians. There is no difference, really, between the wisdom of philosophical awareness—the emphasis of antiquity—and the wisdom of ethical performance—the New Testament emphasis. In any case, it was the common assumption that what is right, true, and proper, the key that unlocks the meaning of life, is within the grasp of anyone who would observe life well and be instructed by the observation of others.

And that is precisely what Job 28 says is impossible. It is an interesting poem which first extols human ingenuity, then forecloses on its capabilities. It also incidentally provides, as a non-theological bonus, some insight into ancient technology.

There is a mine for silver
    and a place for gold, which men refine.
Iron is taken out of the earth,
    copper is smelted from stone.
Men put an end to darkness there,
    they penetrate to the deepest recesses,
    through dark and gloomy rock.
They sink shafts in valleys remote from man,
    forgotten by any human foot,
    they swing suspended, apart from man.
From the earth comes forth bread,
    but underneath it is transformed as by fire.
Its stones are the source of sapphires,
    and its dust contains gold.
This path no bird of prey knows,
    no falcon's eye has descried it.
The proud beasts have not trodden it,
    nor has the lion gone that way.
Only man puts his hand to the flinty rock,
    overturns mountains at their roots.
In the rocks he cuts out channels,
    his eye seeks out every precious thing.
He collects the exudation of the veins,[7]
    and brings hidden things to light (vv 1–11).

Human attainments are impressive, the poet acknowledges, and nowhere more so than in burrowing into the earth to make it give up its hidden treasures of metals and precious stones. Mining was, like navigation in the seas, something practically unknown to the ordinary Israelite and therefore mysterious (cf. Prov 30:18–19 where "the way of a ship on the high seas" is one of those things too wonderful for the sage to understand). Deut 8:9 not withstanding, Palestine was and is a land singularly bereft of mineral resources. Some copper was mined and smelted in the lower Arabah around the Gulf of Aqabah in early Judahite times, but the labor in these forbidding climes and conditions was probably exacted from hapless Edomite subjects. The turquoise mines in the Sinai were famous and very ancient, where Semitic mercenaries in the hire of the Egyptians may just possibly, centuries before the Book of Job, have transformed a few of the Egyptian hieroglyphs into an alphabet that serves us to this day![8] At all events, the poet of Job 28 regards mining as an exotic thing, just as gold, silver, even iron and copper, not to mention sapphires, were exotic in his life. Man has done what none of the other animals has done, invaded the bowels of the earth, venturing where he was never by nature intended to be, bringing light into the subterranean darkness, dropping down into the hollows by ropes, penetrating the recesses and digging shafts where there were none before, burrowing, exploiting, forcing the earth to produce not only its "natural" produce of grain and bread but also to yield its dragon's hoard of precious things.

So much can man do, and so much has he done. But can he do more? Can he solve the real problems of life? Is his technology equal to the task of coping with his spiritual as well as his material dimension? The question that by implication is here being asked is much akin to the implied questions that are today framed in paradigms like: "If we can put a man on the moon, why can't we . . . ?" And the answer of Job 28 is that, unfortunately, we can't.

> But where is wisdom to be found,
>   and where is the place of understanding?
> Man does not know the way to it,
>   nor is it to be found in the land of the living.

The deep says, "It is not in me,"
  and the sea says, "It is not with me."
It cannot be bought by gold,
  nor can silver be weighed for its price.
It cannot be bought with gold of Ophir,
  with precious onyx or with sapphire.
Gold or crystal cannot equal it,
  nor can golden jewelry attain its worth.
Coral and glass are not in question,
  for the price of wisdom is beyond pearls.
The topaz of Ethiopia cannot compare with it,
  nor can it be valued in pure gold.
Whence, then, comes wisdom,
  and where is the place of understanding?
It is hidden from the eyes of all the living,
  and concealed from the birds of the air.
Abaddon and Mot[9] say,
  "Only a rumor have we heard of it."
God it is who understands its way,
  he it is who knows its place (vv 12–23).

Of the concluding verses, vv 24–27 undoubtedly point to the dependence of chap. 28 on the theophany of Job 38–41: the omnipotent God's possession of wisdom is manifest in the intricacies of his creative acts. The final v 28, to the contrary, appears to be a rather clumsy attempt to adjust the message of the poem, after all, to the "standard" wisdom doctrine espoused by Job's friends and Elihu. Not by such a superficial redaction can that deed be done, however, since the verse is plainly of a wholly different mentality from that which has produced all the preceding verses.

What Job 28 professes is exactly the opposite of Proverbs 8, as far as the human attainment of wisdom is concerned. Despite all the human ingenuity which has shown itself capable of exploiting the hidden treasures of the earth, man has not succeeded and cannot succeed in encompassing that wisdom which Prov 8:22 named the very principle and explication of the riddle of things that are. Why is this so? Obviously, because the poet of Job 28 denies that there is any such principle perceptible by man, that there is within his power or purchase any means to cut the Gordian knot that hinders the way to complete understanding. God alone has wisdom, and though his acquisition of wisdom is pictured as essential to the exercise of his creative power (vv 23–27)—as in Proverbs 8, wisdom is figured as a quasi-divine entity coexisting with the creator—he has made use of it but not revealed it in his creation. This conclusion is presented not as a melancholy counsel of despair but simply as a flat statement of inescapable fact: all creatures have limits, and this is one of man's which he must acknowledge if he would inhabit the world of reality rather than of fancy. Blaise Pascal is famous for the aphorism that the God of philosophers is not the God of Christians. The poet who composed Job 28 anticipated Pascal by some centuries. The God of wisdom is not the God of Israel, or—if argumentably the God of Israelite tradition, or some Israelite traditions—not the God of things as they are. Not God, not Israel, not even wisdom itself has been proved inadequate. Wisdom is not denied. It has failed only to the extent that it has not been tried because it could not be tried. The fault was not in the stars, but in those who pretended to read them through a cloudy vision.

Thus, though Job 28 is in all likelihood a redundant addition to the Book of Job as we now have it, out of place certainly and artistically unneeded, it nevertheless forms a splendid preface to the appearance of the Lord and his revelation in chaps. 38–41 to which we shall now, and finally, turn.

Notes

1. The order of verses for these protestations as "restored" by the *New American Bible* and others (vv 5, 7–8, 38–40, 1, 9–34) may make for a more satisfactory development to our tastes, but the verses can also be read in the traditional order. Verses could easily have been misplaced when a line slipped into an adjoining column during manuscript transmission or through the ineptitude of a careless or wrong-headed editor. But it is also always quite possible that biblical authors followed other proprieties of logical development than those which appeal to modern scholars.

2. The exact relationship of the author/editor of Proverbs 1–9 to the rest of the material in this book can be debated; cf. Skehan, "A Single Editor for the Whole Book of Proverbs." Everyone will agree, in any case, that

these chapters are the composition of the book's final editor, whether or not
there were others, and that he did indeed intend that they should serve to
endow Israel's traditional wisdom with divine authority.

3. For the translation and interpretation that follow, see my article,
"Prov. 8:22: Wisdom and Creation," *Journal of Biblical Literature* 99 (1980)
205–216. Cf. also R. B. Y. Scott, *Proverbs. Ecclesiastes* (AB 18, Garden City:
Doubleday, 1965) 68–73.

4. Anyone who feels that this idea is somehow too abstract to have appealed to early Jewish thought should take the trouble to find out something
about early Jewish thought. See Louis Ginzberg, *The Legends of the Jews*
(Philadelphia: Jewish Publication Society, 1968) I, 1–46. Here the personifi-
cation of wisdom is Torah, "with whom God took counsel." See below, Ben
Sira's identification of wisdom and Torah in Sirach 24.

5. Pope, *Job,* xviii.

6. Cf. Franz Hesse, *Hiob* (Zürcher Kommentare AT 14; Zürich: Theo-
logisches Verlag, 1978) 158.

7. Only here, as far as I am aware, do I depart from conventional translations that are given these verses. I am assuming that the mining figure (for
which biblical Hebrew had no technical vocabulary) is being preserved and
therefore that *nĕhārôt,* literally "streams," can be properly rendered "veins"
to denote whence the ore was extracted.

8. Cf. Albert van den Branden, "Nouvel essai du déchiffrement des in-
scriptions protosinaïtiques," *Bibbia e Oriente* 21 (1979) 155–251.

9. Abaddon and Mot are personifications of "Perdition" and "Death."
It was a popular superstition, by no means defunct in our enlightened age,
that the dead possessed knowledge closed off from the living, and that they
could be consulted through various mediums to shed light on the past, present, or future (cf. 1 Sam 28:6–25). Job is saying that neither from this
source nor from any other may man fondly hope to attain that wisdom that
has been entirely foreclosed from him.

8.

AND WHAT DOES
YAHWEH SAY?

In the first place, that Yahweh says anything at all is proof of the failure of wisdom. Eliphaz, Bildad, and Zophar (not to mention the callow Elihu, had he been present) must have been quite as embarrassed as Job himself when the Lord answered Job out of the whirlwind (38:1). Whirlwind—*sĕ'ārâ*—this is the language of theophany, of supernatural intervention, for which there was no place nor need in the scholastic speculation of wisdom. The whirlwind was the vehicle by which the legendary prophet Elijah had been rapt into heaven (2 Kgs 2:1.11) and the way in which Yahweh had appeared to the prophets as well as the way in which they had said that he would appear (cf. Isa 29:6, 40:24, 41:16; Jer 23:19, 30:23; Ezek 1:4, 13:11,13; Zech 9:14). What does this vaguely distasteful flamboyance, this almost vulgar intrusion of the divine presence have to do with the finely chiseled periods with which Job's friends had diagnosed his malady and with which he had rebutted their diagnoses? We are reminded of George Bernard Shaw's *Saint Joan* (not necessarily to be confused, for that matter, with the real Jeanne d'Arc), when Joan reappears only for the discomfiture of both her champions and her traducers.

Job has repeatedly and arrogantly demanded that God be answerable to him. He has appealed from God to a God beyond; he has rested his case with a divine justice in which his traditional God has been found failing; he has rated God an enemy according to this fixed rule of justice and fairness.

> O that I had someone to hear me!
> Here is my sign: Let Shaddai answer me.
> Let my enemy write his indictment (31:35).

But this God whom Job berates is the God of his own mind and that of his friends. There is nothing wrong in such a situation, as we have already seen, since God can only be what we conceive him to be. All that is wrong is that there is no openness to a broader vision, from wherever it may come, in this instance from an experience that transcends prior conviction, the experience of the author of the Book of Job.[1]

At first glance, Yahweh's[2] response to Job in chaps. 38–41[3] seems to be the performance of a God who is merely the caricature of the one against whom Job has complained, a bully fighting a foredoomed battle with superior weapons. "Gird up your loins like a man," says the Lord to Job. "I will question you, and you shall answer me" (38:3). This in conjunction with a preceding verse in which the suggestion has been made that Job has thoroughly muddled the issue with a plethora of words. Is this not Mr. Murdstone fondling the cane as he waits for a stammering David to blurt out inanities?

Actually, it is not. It is, rather, an ironic use of the wisdom technique turned against itself. Was Job present at creation? Does he understand its dimensions and principles, its measurements up, down, and surface, its bounds and limits, its ins and outs, all the other phenomena of nature? Of course he does not. Yet all such happenings of nature were supposed to be the stock in trade of the sages whose business it was to think about such things (cf. 1 Kgs 4:29–34). In other words, Job is being presented by the wisdom instructor (Yahweh) with impossible questions to which he (the wise man) cannot reply. He is being brought to the recognition that there is in the world a rationale of existence that is quite beyond his comprehension.[4]

So it is with the rest of this complex. Even though in chaps. 40–41 Yahweh challenges Job again in much the same words, this time preparatory to confronting him with rather spectacular, even grotesque, evidences of the creative power denied to and totally misunderstood by Job: Behemoth, probably the hippopotamus, and Leviathan, probably the crocodile, the argument is the same. How can Job claim to command a respectable hearing as a man of wisdom in his own constituency if he has failed to make a satisfactory response and can but stand mute?

And stand mute he does, first overtly in 40:3–5, and, somewhat ambiguously, in 42:1–6. Does he really, in this latter passage, take back all that he has said in the preceding chapters? Or does he simply agree that what he said before was said with half-understanding, in view of the more wonderful things that had not yet been revealed to him, and that now he has a new vision of life?

> I talked of things I did not know,
>   things too wonderful for me.
> I have heard of you by hearsay,
>   but now my own eyes have seen you.
> Therefore I despise myself
>   and repent in dust and ashes (42:3.5–6).

No, Job is not repudiating the God-idea entirely, in the sense that there is no purpose in trying to answer the question: "What is God?" Rather, it would appear that now, through his new experience, he wishes to cut the losses of his former speculation and move on to other considerations.[5] Here we must recall the epilogue to the Book of Job, remembering that it is not only a piece of ancient folklore but also the chosen vehicle of the author of this magnificent book:

> Then Yahweh said to Eliphaz the Temanite: "My wrath is kindled against you and your two friends, for you have not spoken seemly to me as has my servant Job. . . . I vow to accept his plea not to deal with you as your folly deserves. For you have not spoken seemly to me as has my servant Job" (42:7–8).

Paradoxically—and of course the Book of Job is quintessentially paradoxical—Job is being praised for having berated the Lord, chal-

lenged him, satirized him, dared him, spurned him. And Eliphaz and
his companions are being rebuked, and more than that, for having
defended God and his justice in every respect. It is quite obvious that
Job without knowing, but with an instinct that reached deeper than
knowledge, had perceived what was true about God, however unpal-
atable it was to him, while Eliphaz and his companions had simply
mouthed platitudes. Wisdom, philosophy, in other words, is pronounced a dead end. At least Job knows this—and possibly his
friends can accept the fact along with him.

No further vision is given. Wisdom has failed. The God who
spoke to Job out of the whirlwind has overwhelmed him with his all-
presence and all-power, but he has offered no path by which man
may seek the divine. The God of the theophany of Job is a *deus ab-
sconditus* even more remote than the God on whom Job refused to
call.

And this is, perhaps, the ultimate paradox of the Book of Job.

Notes

1. Cf. Peter Paul Zarafa, O.P., *The Wisdom of God in the Book of Job*
(Studia Universitatis S. Thomae in Urbe, 8; Rome: Herder, 1978).

2. We note, of course, that now in this response, as in the Prologue and
Epilogue, it is Yahweh of Israel who appears, in distinction to the "wisdom"
surrogates of Eloah, Shaddai, et al., who characterize the dialogue.

3. I am assuming that all these chapters are original to the Book of Job.
See Skehan's "Job's Final Plea (Job 29–31) and the Lord's Reply (Job 38–
41)," *Studies* 114–123.

4. Cf. James G. Williams, "Deciphering the Unspoken: The Theophany of Job," *Hebrew Union College Annual* 49 (1978) 59–72.

5. Cf. P. A. H. de Boer, "Haalt Job bakzeil (Job xlii 6)?" *Nederlands
Theologisch Tijdschrift* 31 (1977) 181–194.

9.

A TRUE PROPHET OF
THE LORD

Let us now turn from wisdom speculation in these times, when ideas were being turned topsy-turvy, when the Book of Ruth could contend with Ezra-Nehemiah or the Book of Deuteronomy, when standard histories and party lines in the Hebrew canon were yet in the making. What was happening with prophecy?

What had already happened to prophecy was fairly evident: it had failed its task. Failed, that is, in the sense that it had given out, was no more. For whatever providential reason, prophecy in Israel was practically coextensive with Israel the independent nation, the nation with king and other institutions firmly established on Israel's own soil. There were great prophets during the exile, it is true, who performed a useful function in fostering Israel's belief in a restoration and, in fact, making that restoration possible. Yet we can hardly believe that the expectations of Jeremiah, of Ezekiel, of the Second Isaiah, or of the anonymous prophets whose words have been incorporated as additions into other prophetic books were quite or adequately realized in the postexilic Jewish community that re-emerged on Palestinian ground. A ground which now, as the province of Yehud, consisted of a few square miles surrounding the city of Jerusalem, at enmity with and in fear of its neighbors, even with its undeniable kinsmen to the north and the south, a province subject to the benign but firm control of the Persian empire, then to the control of a no less foreign and benign Hellenistic suzerainty which at the end became unimaginably demonic, tyrannical, and evil.

Such historical developments point to the second failure of prophecy, that besides petering out it had become incapable of delivering on its promises. The postexilic prophets Haggai and Zechariah had foretold the return of a Davidic messiah-king. He did not appear. Joel foresaw in apocalyptic vision a Jerusalem which would be a new center of the world for all of its redeemed, before which all other nations would cringe and pay homage. How little like this was the province of Yehud, repopulated by *revenants* only after considerable armtwisting on the part of Zionist zealots, the Second Temple, a sad contrast with the former temple of Solomon's glory (Ezra 3:12–13), and the city of Jerusalem itself, precariously rebuilt as a walled (and therefore precariously autonomous) entity (Neh 2:3–17). Obadiah and other voices that have been interpolated into preexilic and postexilic prophets alike, which, in fact, did not even need to be interpolated, since the prophecy was already there (cf. Ezek 37:15–22), confidently looked forward to a total restoration of the vanished Golden Age when Israel and Judah would be reunited under a Davidic king as in the days of David and Solomon. Of course, nothing like this ever happened, not even anything that could be construed as approximate to it. (The only exception to this statement could be found in the events that succeeded 175 B.C., when the Maccabean revolt against Seleucid tyranny provoked and resulted in a brief period of Jewish imperialism—including forced conversion and territorial aggrandizement—that lasted, with steady deteriorations, till the *pax romana* of 63 B.C. But these developments have nothing to do with our present concerns.) The last prophet in the Hebrew Old Testament who bears a name is Malachi, and his is not really a name but a designation borrowed from 3:1, "my messenger." Malachi is, therefore, another anonymous contender in the lists to speak up for what he thought was right and proper. What he thought was right and proper, evidently, were the virtues which Ezra and Nehemiah were trying to enforce. He recognizes the existence of some obvious abuses ritual, professional, and social—but who needs prophetic inspiration to denounce such paltry derelictions? All this now having been taken into account, let us now consider what the beginning of the Book of Jonah meant when it was first composed. One can be sure, first of all, that it would not have been sympathetic to prophecy. By this time prophecy had become, or was fast on the way of becoming, only a

dim and somewhat flawed memory, evoking the fortuneteller or sha-
man image that it possesses for many contemporary minds (note the
instructive passage in 2 Maccabees 2).

The book begins:

> *1:1 So did the word of Yahweh come about to Jonah ben Amit-*
> *tai:*
> *2 "Get up and go to Nineveh the great city, and call out against*
> *3 it, for their evil has come to my attention." Jonah did get up,*
> *but only to flee far-westward,[1] anywhere away from Yahweh.*
> *He went down to Jaffa, found a ship bound for the far west,*
> *paid the fare, and boarded it in order to go with them far-*
> *westward, anywhere away from Yahweh.*

Jonah ben Amittai: the point is often made by commentators[2]
that this name, etymologically, is probably something like "Dove,
the son of Faithfulness" (or, "Truth"). It is possible, in view of what
follows, that the author does enjoy a bit of irony in this direction, in
the manner of James Joyce or, say, Saul Bellow's Mr. Sammler. It is
less likely, I suspect, that a connection was being suggested with the
city of Nineveh, sacred to the goddess Ishtar, whose fertility symbols
were often the dove or a fish (2:1 and following: for good measure,
nun in Aramaic and late Hebrew meant "fish"!). The satire of the
author of Jonah is already adequately accounted for by the fact that
there was, indeed, or had been, a prophet named Jonah ben Amittai.
He appears quite briefly in 2 Kgs 14:25, a memory from the time of
King Jeroboam II of Israel (786–746 B.C.), obviously as a nationalistic prophet, a prophet of the court, who had encouraged Jeroboam to
"restore," i.e., reconquer, the ancient boundaries of Israel in the
name of the Lord. This original Jonah was a native of Gath-hepher,
a town in the northern territory of Zebulon (Josh 19:13). That a
prophet of this stamp should be chosen as the anti-hero of this story
is a premonition of the parody that will follow. A prophet like Jonah
ben Amittai, had he been true to type, would have leaped at the op-
portunity to call down doom on Nineveh. Witness the prophecy of
Nahum, the work of another nationalistic prophet, who can obviously not restrain his glee over the imminent destruction of that city by
the Babylonians in 612 B.C.

Nineveh, the ultimate capital of the Assyrian empire, is frequently called in the Book of Jonah "the great city." That it was, as
archeology has revealed, though hardly of quite the dimensions with
which legend had endowed it according to Jonah 3:3. Engagingly,
one of the two great mounds that now partially conceal that ancient
site near the modern city of Mosul in northern Iraq is known to the
Arabs as Nebi Yunus—"the prophet Jonah"—and there is a convenient "tomb" of Jonah nearby.[3] As it figures in our present concern,
Nineveh, capital of the great power that had put an end to the northern kingdom of Israel in 721 B.C. and had devastated and subjugated
the southern kingdom of Judah as well, was now emblematic of *the*
great city that was inimical to Yahweh, to his people, and his purposes—much as Babylon and Rome would later appear in Jewish
and Christian symbolics. When the Book of Judith figured an incur-
sion into the peaceable kingdom of a totally theological and unhistorical Israel by those who were to serve as foils for the delineation of an
ideal Jewish heroine (Judith = Jewess), the archvillain of the piece,
or at least the archvillain who pulls the strings, is portrayed as Nebuchadnezzar—that is, Nebuchadnezzar II, the Chaldean king who destroyed Jerusalem in 586 B.C.—and he is said, in a flat contradiction
of history, since indeed he put an end to the Assyrian empire, to be
the ruler of the Assyrians in "the great city" of Nineveh (Jdt 1:1).

Why does Jonah refuse the mission of the Lord and try to evade
him at all costs? In 4:2 he makes his own answer, but that is far after
the fact, and by the time we have reached this verse we have little
confidence in Jonah's self-justification. We may suspect, therefore,
that the author of this book is asking us to consider the incongruity
of a dutiful prophet, ordained by destiny to do precisely what he is
inspired to do in respect to that most sinful of all cities, instead refusing the mission as though he were one of those errant prophets of old
like Micaiah ben Imlah (cf. 1 Kgs 22:5–28). It is an action totally out
of character. And for the author of the Book of Jonah we can probably conclude that it was all one: prophecy no longer mattered much,
whether it was for good or for ill.

> 4 *Then Yahweh blew up a great wind over the sea so that a great*
> *tempest raged in the sea and the ship was on the point of crack-*

5 ing up. The sailors were afraid, and each one cried out to his
god. They jettisoned the ship's cargo into the sea in order to
lighten it under them. But Jonah had gone down into the hold
of the craft, had lain down, and had fallen fast asleep. The
6 captain found him there and cried, "What are you doing there
asleep? Get up, call to your god! Perhaps this god will take
heed of us so that we don't perish."

An extraordinary scene. All of a sudden we are *in medias res,* no
transitions given, no stage directions. Biblical narrative is less interested in dramatic peripateia than it is in making its point. The scene
dissolves in which we saw Jonah laying down his shekels and book-
ing his passage into this one when the captain (harassed by other un-
mentioned scenes that have already taken place on deck), shakes the
slumbering prophet (prophet!) awake and demands that he make an
account of himself.

According to v 4 it is the Lord that has stirred up this storm and
imperiled the ship, but only the pagan sailors and their captain have
got a glimmer of this fact and have taken what remedies they know
to avoid disaster. This contrast is made all the more poignant by the
choice of words made by the author. The "sleep," whether as verb or
noun, which is ascribed to Jonah in this passage does not simply refer to that which stitches up the ravelled sleeve of care but is, in the
Hebrew, almost always a quasi-technical term for the sleep induced
by God through which revelation comes (Gen 2:21, 15:12; Job 4:13,
33:15; Isa 29:10; Dan 8:18, 10:9–10). Here is a prophet of the Lord—
mark him well—full in the possession of a divine mission entrusted
to him, who can only dissemble the word that is being revealed within him and pretend to drowse away while all the world that matters
about him is being shattered to pieces.

7 Then they said to one another: "Come on, let's cast lots and
find out who is responsible for this evil that has fallen on us."
8 They cast lots, and the lot fell against Jonah. Then they said
to him: "For god's sake, tell us who is responsible for this evil
that has fallen upon us. What is your business, and where do
you come from? What is your country and of what nationality

> 9 are you?" He told them, "I am a Hebrew, and I fear Yahweh
>   the God of the heavens, who made the sea and the dry land."
> 10 Then the crew felt a great fear, and they said to him: "What
>   have you done?" For the crew knew that he was fleeing some-
>   where away from Yahweh, now that he had told them so.

Again the scene shifts. All of a sudden Jonah is on deck amidst
the crew and taking his chances on who will be scapegoat of this mis-
adventure, a scapegoat which is to be determined by lot. The captain
has disappeared, and we now have a drumhead court. Superstition
reigns, but probably the result of the lot-casting is foreordained, all
the same. According to the current wisdom, such an unusual storm
at sea must be the effect of an angry god of the elements. The sailors,
proverbially a cautious and self-preserving lot when confronted by
the indescribable hazards of the sea, would have known that their
personal tutelary deities were properly placated and satisfied: the
necessary insurance premiums were paid up in full. It must be, then,
that whatever was wrong was the fault of the stranger in their midst,
apparently the sole passenger that they had on board.

Jonah is quite helpful, and a trifle selective, in responding to the
sailors' inquisition. What is his country and nationality? He is a Hebrew: in these days, "Hebrew" was the term used by Jews to identify
themselves to others, since it was the term by which others knew
them (so Gen 14:13, 40:15; Exod 2:7, etc.). So might a modern-day
subject of Her Britannic Majesty own up, reluctantly, to being a
"Britisher," a citizen of the Fifth Republic acknowledge that he is a
"Frenchie," or a foreign-born native of the Old Dominion confess,
with a high degree of puzzlement, that he is indeed a "Yank." Implicitly, Jonah also answers the question as to who is responsible for
the evil that had fallen upon them, since the question was being
asked in the context of avenging deity. Though Jonah is an apostate
from his calling and his religious profession, the sailors force from
him a full profession of his faith. "I fear Yahweh the God of the
heavens, who made the sea and the dry land." "The God of the heavens" was a designation which the Jews had picked up from their Persian overlords to designate the supreme God (2 Chr 36:23; Ezra 1:2;
Dan 2:18, etc.). In the context it is a most happy designation, since in
the author's purview the sailors are doubtless Phoenicians—those

strange northern folk who so often deserted the certain ways to venture out on the sea in ships—whose chief deity was *Ba'al šamêm*, "lord of the heavens" (the Hellenistic Zeus Olympios, disfigured into the "horrible abomination" of 1 Macc 1:54). Jonah also adds the helpful note that it is he who made the sea and the dry land, as though to remove any further doubt as to what god has engaged to take on their fragile little craft in a personal vendetta.

Jonah does not answer the question: "What is your business?" He does not need to, for it has already been answered to the satisfaction of the sailors. He is obviously in rebellion against the direction of this mighty God, whatever he may be pretending to do. Hence their final actions:

> 11 *So they asked him: "What shall we do with you, so that the sea may calm down under us?" For the sea was increasingly tempestuous. He told them: "Take me up and throw me into*
> 12 *the sea. Then the sea will calm down under you. For I know that I am responsible for this great tempest having come upon you."*
> 13 *The crew took to the oars trying to get back to the dry land, but they could not, because the sea was increasingly tempestuous against them. So they called to Yahweh, crying out,*
> 14 *"Please, Yahweh, don't make us perish for the life of this man, and don't hold us guilty of an innocent man's death, for you, Yahweh, have brought it all about just as you pleased."*
> 15 *Then they took up Jonah and threw him into the sea, and the sea left off its raging. The crew then felt a great fear of Yah-*
> 16 *weh, and they offered sacrifices to Yahweh and made vows.*

There is some beautiful satire here. In the first place the Yahweh whom Jonah has introduced to his pagan companions in the animistic terms with which they were familiar now proceeds to act as though he were indeed an animistic spirit. He will not be placated until he is given a human sacrifice. Nothing could be farther remote in the religious philosophy of postexilic Judaism from what constituted true religion than a throw-back of this kind, which Jonah "the prophet" cheerfully accepts as matter-of-fact in v 12. The pagan sailors evince a far more sophisticated and elevated perception of the nature of deity in v 13: God helps those who help themselves. They are in no respect eager to abandon Jonah to the waves, whatever may be the strange will of this god that is driving him on. They make every effort to save him, every effort they can to save themselves by the same means, and only at the end do they have to succumb to fate, which is a tragic theme that is hardly Israelite.[4] To sacrifice a human being for a greater good, or a common good, is alien to Israelite thought. Centuries ago Israel's ancestors had shed themselves of this terrible superstitious blight. Yet here, in this pseudo-prophetic passage, Yahweh is represented as requiring just such a thing, a requirement affirmed by his prophet, resisted and only reluctantly acceded to by pagans who feel that the whole thing is wrong, whose better instincts are simply overwhelmed by a force they cannot resist, morally or otherwise.

Israel was uncertain in these times. That Gentiles should have "felt a great fear of Yahweh" and "offered sacrifices to Yahweh and made vows" was not necessarily a positive response as far as the author of Jonah was concerned. They could have been feeding a retrograde religion. Isa 66:18–21 portrays the then "establishment" view of the future:

> I come to gather all nations and tongues . . . they shall come and see my glory . . . and they shall proclaim my glory among the nations. . . . They shall proclaim my glory among the nations as an offering to the Lord . . . just as the Israelites bring their offerings to the house of the Lord. . . . Some of these I will take as priests and Levites, says the Lord.

Obviously this author thinks of the Gentiles as peoples who can be comfortably assimilated to Israel. The author of Jonah, on the other hand, perhaps thought that the Gentiles should be framing the questions for Israel (like the author of the Wisdom of Solomon?). In sum, the final v 16 is probably not climax but rather comic relief: sacrificing to Yahweh and making vows to him may have been the absolute contradiction of all that was intended by the author of the Book of Jonah.

Notes

1. "Far-westward" or "the far west" here translates "(to) Tarshish," a place name of Phoenician origin ("refinery"?) probably referring to various commercial ports along the Mediterranean littoral (cf. Isa 23:10; Ezek 38:13; Ps 72:10, etc.). For a Palestinian Jew of the time of Jonah Tarshish was simply one of those faraway places with strange-sounding names, not unlike Timbuktu for an average English-speaker nowadays, somewhere across the Great Sea, which always remained for the landbound Palestinians the barrier to the west.

2. Recently by John C. Holbert, " 'Deliverance Belongs to Yahweh!': Satire in the Book of Jonah," *Journal for the Study of the Old Testament* 21 (1981) 59–81.

3. Jonah was an Old Testament figure who captivated the imagination of the Prophet Muhammad, and he is featured in the Qur'ān as an "apostle" and as "the one in the fish" (*suras* 6:86, 10:98, 37:139, 48:48).

4. The tragic theme has been suppressed in Israelite historiography in view of its conflict with what has generally been assimilated under the designation "providence." Exceptions peep through the sources, perhaps no better exemplified than in the tragic history of Saul, which can still be discerned through Judahite redaction and revisionism. Cf. W. Lee Humphreys, "The Rise and Fall of King Saul: A Study of Ancient Narrative Stratum in 1 Samuel," *Journal for the Study of the Old Testament* 18 (1980) 74–90; N. Poulssen, "Saul in Endor (1 Sam. 28). Een peiling naar de verte van God en het zoeken van de mens," *Tijdschrift voor Theologie* 20 (1980) 133–160.

10.

THE MAN IN THE GREAT FISH

There was a time, now happily buried in a history of the past needing no remembrance, when the credibility of the Book of Jonah was thought to depend on the historical verisimilitude of what is described in its second chapter. As recently as 1961 the late Alberto Vaccari, S.J., one of the most distinguished and honored philologists whom Italy ever produced and the mentor of many at the Pontifical Biblical Institute in Rome, felt called upon to publish a spirited defense of the historicity of the Book of Jonah, largely because he thought that the typology of the Jonah-figure exploited by the New Testament and ascribed by it to the authority of Jesus himself (Matt 12:39–41, etc.) required for its validity nothing short of statistical historical reality.[1] Vaccari's was an article of sufficient weight to require of André Feuillet, author of several articles in *Revue biblique* which he had subsumed into an article on Jonah in the *Dictionnaire de la Bible Supplément*—works which Vaccari had singled out as particularly deplorable—a "mise au point" in which he had to defend the critical view of this book which he had espoused.[2]

That the Book of Jonah became in popular acclaim a whale of a story is, of course, another result of misdirected historicism. Since the available taxonomy of fishes provided little encouragement to earnest seekers measuring for suitable if temporary lodging for an average-sized Jew, it was concluded early on that the host-beast must have been a whale. No matter that the whale is no fish but one of our distant mammalian cousins: even Herman Melville, who acquired some reputation in matters whalish, persistently and perversely makes out Moby Dick and his colleagues to have been big fish. A sad corollary of this cetacean mistake was the "whale pulpit,"[3] a baroque monstrosity which must rank as the consummate realization of vulgarity through the foreordained marriage of artistic bad taste with theological bad taste.

To be sure, in this post-"Jaws" age we know, if we did not know before, that the shark, with perfect ichthyological credentials, can do as a fish what our predecessors thought that only a whale could do. Still, when we consider the feeding habits of the great white, we can hardly credit that the Lord who "provided for" this great fish to swallow Jonah, just as he later "provided for," in sequence, a leafy plant, a worm, and a burning east wind (4:6–8) for Jonah's further instruction, could have had in mind that machine of perpetual motion which has no apparent function except to eat: beyond those great triangular teeth there would have been no room for a whole, psalm-singing prophet. In other words, there is absolutely no point in trying to extract some grain of facticity out of this obviously fanciful story. Jonah's credibility lies in its religious and philosophical message, not in its contribution to biological enigmas.

The present writer has never thought that the picture of Jonah in the belly of the fish, given the basic premise of this never-neverland of symbolism, was quite as unbelievable as what we are invited to believe that Jonah did in this situation, that is, deliver himself of a hymn of thanksgiving, totally out of character and totally unreal in the circumstances. (Did it take Jonah three days to recite his hymn?) Look at 2:1–2,11:

> *2:1 Yahweh provided for a great fish to swallow Jonah, and Jonah stayed in the belly of the fish for three days and three nights.*
>
> *2 Then Jonah prayed to Yahweh his God from the belly of the fish,*
>
> *11 and Yahweh commanded the fish, and it spewed Jonah out on the dry land.*

Quite evidently the psalm of Jonah in vv 3–10 can be withdrawn from its context without disruption, as long as we are persuaded that it is superfluous to the narrative, adds nothing to it, and is only the luxury which a later expansive and imaginative editor permitted himself. Many scholars have so concluded. But there is reason to think that they were wrong.[4]

It is easy to think that they are wrong, for Jonah's psalm is so much in character with this parody of a prophet that the psalm would have had to be invented—was?—had it not been original to the thought of the author. Here is the clumsiest of all the prophets, commanded to go to the east and fleeing to the far west, called from slumber to his charismatic duty by a bluff pagan captain, awakened to his proximate duty by superstitious sailors who are at the same time courteous, solicitous, and unwilling to offend, cast in the sea at his own disposal, miraculously engulfed, miraculously disgorged. Are we to imagine that this Jonah has learnt a single thing from this abortive journey to the far west, wherever we may be expected to believe that he was spewed up on some Mediterranean shore? Probably not. Jonah is what Jonah was, and as Jonah will prove himself to be in chaps. 3–4 of the Book of Jonah.

And therefore we conclude that the Jonah of 2:3–10 is an original construct of the author of this book. Jonah is not only a failed prophet, as all prophecy is failed to some degree,[5] he has become for our author almost a buffoon of prophecy, and therefore an *opera buffa di profezia,* carrying with it the caricature and the debasement of the Greek chorus which Aristophanes had already committed in his "comedies." Aristophanes, we remember, was writing just about at this same time on the other side of the Aegean. For what we are presented with in 2:3–10 is a hymn of confidence and thanksgiving, totally out of character of the Jonah thus far presented and totally out of the character of the literary form—plea, lamentation, confession—that we might expect to find at this juncture. Truly, Jonah is being ridiculed here as before and in what follows: what he says must be construed as meaningless as far as his own *persona* is concerned, however precious the thoughts are that have been preserved in this poem.

The poem is a pastiche of Psalm verses, which are indicated in the right-hand column. They have nothing to do with the "historical" character of the prophet Jonah. They have a great deal to do with what the author of this book thought were valuable spiritual insights:

> 3 "I called out, out of all my anguish,   *Pss 18:7, 120:1*
>   unto Yahweh, and he answered me.
>   From the depths of Sheol I cried
>   and you listened to my voice.
> 4 When you cast me to the deep,
>   [in the heart of the waves,]
>   and the torrent swirled about me,
>   every breaker and billow of yours   *Ps 42:8*
>   was washing over me;
> 5 then I said, 'I have been banished   *Ps 31:23*
>   from the sight of your eyes,
>   yet fain would I gaze once more
>   on the temple of your holiness.'
> 6 The waters engulfed me up to my neck,   *Pss 18:5, 69:2*
>   the abyss surrounded me,
>   seaweed twined about my head.
> 7 To the roots of the mountains,   *Ps 16:1b*
>   to the bourne I went down,
>   its bars were closing upon me forever,
>   but you brought back my life from the pit,   *Ps 30:4*
>   O Yahweh my God!
> 8 When the breath was stifling within me *Pss 5:8, 18:7, 89:3*
>   I remembered Yahweh;
>   my lament came through to you,
>   to the temple of your holiness.
> 9 Those who worship vain idols   *Ps 31:7*
>   throw away their hope for mercy.
> 10 But I, to the sound of thanksgiving,   *Ps 50:14, etc.*
>   will offer my sacrifice to you.
>   What I have vowed I shall fulfill:
>   salvation is from Yahweh!"

If one would like to pursue this poem into its structure, it might be difficult to discover a central theme that would give the key to

what is the ultimate thrust of the passage. On the one hand, the She-
ol of Yahweh, the depths of v 3, correspond with the triumphalist
victory of v 10, in which the client of the Lord, assured of salvation,
duly proffers his vowed offerings for the relief that has been given
him. In this contribution, is there any correspondence between v 4,
"the breakers of death" from which the faithful of the Lord confidently hope to be delivered,[6] and the total absence of hope that
awaits idolaters according to v 9? One might doubt this, but then
again, there is reason to suspect that the suddenly pious Jonah is a
perfect foil for the despised idolaters—the captain and his crew, in
this instance—who have by casting him into the deep forced him to
recognize and call upon his own God. The correspondence of vv 5
and 8 is more obvious: joined by the theme of "the temple of your
holiness," the self-banished one through remembrance of Yahweh—
a remembrance effected through the fairly bluff but also not unsym-
pathetic measures of his pagan fellow-travelers—is brought to com-
munion with God in that ultimate act of faith that finds expression in
lamentation. For lamentation, like the cry of the poor and downtrodden for redress (and indeed, lamentation is quintessentially the cry of
the poor and downtrodden for redress), is an appeal to what lies beyond what is juridically expected, to a dispensation that dispenses
with the norms of justice as men understand justice. Finally, we consider vv 6–7. Each verse speaks of the depths: in v 6 the psalmist is
there in despond, but in v 7 he is brought forth therefrom, from She-
ol, the pit, the waters of death, through God's mercy.

The structure we have been discerning here in the foregoing
verses is sometimes called *chiasmus,* because in its construction it
vaguely resembles a Greek *chi* ("X" in our alphabet), setting up a
correspondence between acceding and receding elements of an argument that converge at the center to make their point. Actually, chiasmus is never necessarily a studied literary form, since it is almost
inevitable in the common logic of communication that a position will
be set forth a. b. c. and then, the point made, summation or confirmation will be registered as c. b. a. At the same time, *chiasmus* is
definitely a studied form frequently in the Bible, and in a book like
that of Jonah where hardly anything is ever done by chance, we
should not rule out the likelihood that it has in fact been intended in
Jonah 2:3–10. Furthermore, there is no "X" juncture here, no mid-

dle point toward which the a. b. c. should lead and from which the c. b. a. should recede. This fact does not argue against but rather argues in favor of the presence of a studied *chiasmus* here, in the context of the Book of Jonah. For the point that is being made in respect to Jonah's lament is that the lament really has no point.

Consider what we would be expected to believe, were we to take this psalm at its face value, the prayer of a humble and dutiful servant of the Lord, persecuted for his fidelity and eschewing the beguilements of idolatrous pagans, a man beset by a contrary world of which he had had no part in the making, steadfast in his trust in the inscrutable designs of God. Is this the Jonah of our chap. 1? Obviously not. More importantly, is this the Jonah of chaps. 3–4 whom we are shortly to see? Again, obviously not. In the psalm of chap. 2 we see no sudden conversion to the divine will and dispensation of a recalcitrant servant of the Lord who now prefers that will to his own. Jonah has not changed, but he has dissembled. He has mawkishly adopted as his own and without feeling some of the most poignant utterances of the Lord's own true believers. He is not only a failed prophet, a caricature of prophecy, he is also a mockery of Israelite piety.

Chap. 2 of the Book of Jonah is, therefore, on the balance by no means an intrusion into the author's text but rather an integral part of his sardonic reflection on a still venerated institution of the irrecoverable past which had sadly failed its mission. The author of Jonah will not be content to condemn prophecy as failed and inefficacious. He also wants to assert that its final practitioners had become small, mean, grubby, and hypocritical.

Notes

1. His "Il genere letterario del libro di Giona in recenti pubblicazioni" (pp. 28) published widespread by the Lateran University as an "Omaggio dell'autore" was an abstract from *Divinitas* 5 (1961).

2. Feuillet's defense appeared in an "Avis au lecteur" inserted into a subsequent fascicule of the *Supplément* (a collection still in process of publication, the most recent contribution having appeared in 1981). Feuillet's article was featured in vol. 4 (1949), cols. 1104–1131. In his "Avis" he defends

his position alleging (1) that his thought had been distorted, (2) that it was nevertheless more faithful to the biblical text than that of his detractors, and (3) that it avoided conclusions that would call down ridicule on Catholic exegesis.

3. A particularly hideous example of a "whale-pulpit" is the sole illustration of a book by Hans Walter Wolff, *Jonah: Church in Revolt* (St. Louis: Clayton Publishing House, 1978). The German antecedents of this work are somewhat unclear. See the review in *Old Testament Abstracts* 1 (1978) 294.

4. Cf. Holbert, n. 2 in the preceding chapter.

5. See Robert P. Carroll, *When Prophecy Failed: Cognitive Dissonance in the Prophetic Traditions of the Old Testament* (A Crossroad Book; New York: Seabury, 1979).

6. Cf. Bruce Vawter, C.M., "A Note on 'The Waters Beneath the Earth,' " *Catholic Biblical Quarterly* 22 (1960) 71–73.

11.

SURELY, THE GREATEST OF ALL PROPHETS

3:1 So again did the word of Yahweh come about to Jonah:
2 "Get up, and go to Nineveh the great city and call unto it the
3 proclamation I am telling you." So Jonah got up and went
to Nineveh. Now Nineveh was an incredibly great city, a
4 three-days' walk in expanse. Jonah began his walk through
the city, and after one day's walk he called out, saying,
5 "Forty days more and Nineveh will be overthrown!" The peo-
ple of Nineveh believed God: they proclaimed a fast and put
6 on sackcloth, from the greatest to the least of them. And
when the news reached the king of Nineveh, he rose from his
throne, took off his robe, donned sackcloth, and sat on the
city dump.
7 Then he had this proclamation published in Nineveh: "By de-
cree of the king and his nobles: Let neither man nor beast,
neither cattle nor flock, touch anything; let them neither take
food nor drink water. But let them don sackcloth, both man
8 and beast, and call out to God mightily; and let each one
turn away from his evil way and the violence they are doing.
9 Who knows, God may turn away and show mercy, he may
desist from his fierce anger, and we may not perish!"

Marvel of marvels! This chapter might well be called: Jonah
changes his mind. Whatever it is to be called, the passage we now

take up continues to portray Jonah as a comic character and slow
learner. On what dry land Jonah was spewed out by the great fish,
we are not told explicitly. We may be sure, however, that the author
intended us to understand that the scene of this prophetic regurgita-
tion is the same as that of Yahweh's first summons to the prophet,
now reiterated after the tiresome and ludicrous entr'acte provoked
by Jonah's foolish flight. That is to say, we are certainly back in Palestine, the land of Israel and of Israel's God. Jonah's flight to the far
west, anywhere away from Yahweh, reflects an antiquated and su-
perseded theology, a source of amusement to the author of Jonah,
which restricted the power and activity of a national god—and remember, the historical Jonah ben Amittai was a prophet of a national god—to his own solid turf and constituency. (Recall the story in 2
Kgs 5:17–18, where a grateful Naaman begs a portion of the soil of
Palestine to carry back with him to Syria, that upon it in his own
homeland he may properly worship Yahweh rather than Rimmon,
the god of Syria.)

The interlude of chap. 2 has at least disabused Jonah of his insu-
lar concept of the scope of Yahweh's jurisdiction. Fleeing the land of
Israel had availed him nothing, for the God of Israel had been able to
single him out and pluck him from the hold of a ship on the high seas
and to provide him with unusual transport back to the place of his
origin. That Jonah now accedes to a divine call that he had previous-
ly spurned does not, therefore, register any conversion on his part
but rather and simply his acquiescence to the *force majeure* of a God
whose commands, however quixotic and erratic, he has no power to
resist.

And so he goes to Nineveh, "the great city." There was an element in Israel, as doubtless there has been an element in every society down to present ones, which regarded "the city" as the enemy of
homespun virtues, the sewer into which every maleficent political
humor was allowed to flow, something like the "wen" of William
Cobbett. It was an element, but an element that has been greatly exaggerated as respects the biblical chronicle, in obedience to a supposed "nomadic ideal" that has probably been more in the eye of the
beholder than of the one beheld.[1] Nothing deleterious is said about
Nineveh in the Book of Jonah; on the contrary, it is presented as a
model of prompt obedience to the divine word. This, too, of course,

is part and parcel of Jonah's irony and sarcasm. As we have already remarked, the Book of Judith, an allegorical short story of the inter-testamental period, identified Nineveh (quite unhistorically, of course) as the capital city of (the equally unhistorical, in this context) Nebuchadnezzar, "king of the Assyrians," the quintessential enemies of Israel. Such names are pure ciphers, evocative of ancient historical memories but indicative of no real contemporary history. And as these were in the Book of Judith, so "Nineveh" already was in the Book of Jonah.

A statistical note is struck: "Nineveh was an incredibly great city, a three-days walk in expanse." Quite literally, the Hebrew text reads "a city great unto God," a superlative that is certainly approximated by our colloquial "godawfully big." There is no point, of course, in trying to retrieve history again out of the "three-days walk" of its extent, by imagining that the biblical author meant the circumference of Nineveh rather than its diameter, for example, or some similar subterfuge. By Palestinian standards Nineveh had doubtless become legendary as *the* great city, but anyone who has wandered through its imposing ruins in what is now northern Iraq knows that a half hour's saunter would have been sufficient to exhaust its possibilities from stem to stern, however winding may have been its cardinal streets. It was no Tokyo, nor Paris, nor Manhattan, nor Chicago, nor London, nor Sydney—any of which can easily be traversed by a resolute walker in a small fraction of three days. We make both ourselves and the Bible ridiculous when we try to make of its humor and flights of fancy mere dry statistics.

We do not ask how Jonah got to Nineveh: in grim fact a laborious journey north from Palestine over the hump of the Fertile Crescent and then down the valley of the Tigris River. We are not told why Jonah delayed proclaiming his message to the Ninevites till he had traversed a third of their city: was he now considered to be in its very heart? What we are told is an astounding thing which, were it literal fact, would certify Jonah to be not only the greatest—if to be successful is to be great—of all God's prophets, but also the most efficacious missionary who ever summoned sinners to the mercy seat. "Forty days more and Nineveh will be overthrown!" is not even a summons; it is a statement of fact, a proclamation of doom, confronting the hearer with a judgment to which there is no appeal, unless it be the appeal of a contrite soul who cries for mercy against justice. The author must have had in mind the similar words of doom of prophets like Amos, Micah, Jeremiah—words which fell on deaf ears in Israel and Judah and as a result constituted these prophets "failures." In bitter contrast, these despised Ninevites. "Forty days more and Nineveh will be overthrown": eight words in English, only five in the Hebrew text. Truly a sermon of commendable economy. The Greek Septuagint, for some reason, has turned the forty days of v 4 into three. Three or forty, each had symbolic potential for an Israelite reader.

Now, in contradiction to the Israelite experience of doom prophecy, the Ninevites "believed God": the same expression is used of the great act of faith of Abraham in Gen 15:6. They need no prompting, no inducements, no introduction to or conversion to the God of Israel—again we are expected to suspend historical verisimilitude. They simply repent, as though they were all devout Jews cognizant of devout Jewish practices, and call for mercy. In v 5 it appears that the people of Nineveh anticipate their king—who would he have been in the mind of the author of Jonah? perhaps Nebuchadnezzar again? Sargon? Sennacherib?—in initiating the rites of penitence. The Ninevites "proclaimed a fast," like the Jerusalemites of Jer 36:9, "from the greatest to the least" (the reverse of a Jeremian formula, in Jer 6:13 and repeatedly "from the least to the greatest"), but unlike the Judahite king who refused to be moved by the popular fast or to join in it, but rather spurned the prophet's words with the utmost contempt and disdain (Jer 36:20–26), the king of Nineveh imitates the "patient" Job (Job 2:8) and assumes a penitential posture upon the city dump.

The king of Nineveh, unlike the king of Judah who refused to hear his nobles, involves them with himself in a royal decree by which he catches up with the people of whom he is the leader and succeeds in surpassing them. Not only does he endorse the penitential measures that have been proclaimed "from the greatest to the least"—men, women, and children of all classes—he extends them to man and beast, cattle and flock, in short to every living creature. Partly we may be again confronted by the author's antic wit: it is easy enough to deprive domestic animals of fodder and drink and thus pretend that they are "fasting," but it is another thing to imagine cow or ewe parading about in sackcloth. Yet it is not the humor of mockery that drives the author; it continues to be the humor of parody.

We have already seen more than one instance in which the author of Jonah seems to be making deliberate allusions to the prophecy of Jeremiah. These continue in Jonah 3:7–9. "Man and beast" in Jeremiah is a standard formula for the whole of a given society, be it the object of God's creation, of his beneficence, or of his condemnation (see Jer 7:20, 21:6, 27:5, 31:27, 32:43, 33:10). That each of these should turn away from his separate evils and wrongdoings is likewise the echo of a Jeremian formula (see Jer 25:5, 26:3, 36:3.7, etc.). As for the wistful and somewhat wan hope that God might turn away from his fierce anger, repent, and show mercy, the most obvious prophetic allusion is in the late Book of Joel 2:14, though an earlier precedent might be found in Amos 5:15, even though less obviously. Yahweh's "fierce anger" is another Jeremian catch-phrase (Jer 4:8, 26, 12:13, 25:37,38, 30:24, 51:45). There can be no doubt that the author of Jonah has been indulging throughout in a gentle mockery of traditional prophetic language.

The point of it all is revealed in what follows. For whereas supposedly faithful Judahites had proclaimed a fast in vain to stay the hand of divine retribution, the flamboyant penitential rites of supposedly infidel Ninevites are countered by an equally extravagant action of God which shows all too clearly in contrast how efficacious they were.

It should be noted and filed for future reference that the burden of Yahweh's message to Nineveh through Jonah regards moral conduct and says nothing at all about what a contemporary postexilic Jewish critic would have been expected to find reprehensible in this epitome of the heathen world: idolatry and such vain worship. Jonah speaks *to* the Gentiles in terms that an earlier prophet (Amos 1:3–2:3) spoke, without reflection, *about* them: as people responsible to and responsive to the same moral standards that were expected of the people of Israel's God. There is no call to the Ninevites to conform to the religion of Israel, no hint of proselytism, as in the truly ecumenical thought of the Third Isaiah (Isa 66:18–21, for example).[2] Not by accident, too, is it that after v 1 of Jonah 3, the specifically Israelite divine name "Yahweh" does not appear, but always the generic "God." Eminently proper on the lips of the Ninevites who knew not Yahweh, it is singular and significant from the author of Jonah to identify him who spoke to the Ninevites and revealed to them his moral imperatives.

Notes

1. Cf. Frank S. Frick, *The City in Ancient Israel* (Society of Biblical Literature Dissertation Series, 36; Missoula: Scholars Press, 1977).

2. At the other extreme of Jonah is the doctrine of Baruch, who echoes the language of Trito-Isaiah but excludes Gentiles forever from God's glory. Cf. Frederic Raurell, " 'Doxa' i particularisme nacionalista en Ba 4, 5–5, 9," *Revista Catalana de Teologia* 5 (1980) 265–295.

12.

GOD CHANGES HIS MIND

10 When God saw what they had done, turning away from their
evil ways, then God repented of the evil he had said he would
do to them, and he did not do it.
4:1 Now this afflicted Jonah like a great evil, and he became an-
2 gry. He appealed to Yahweh: "If you please, Yahweh, didn't
I say this would happen when I was still in my native land? It
was for this reason I tried to flee far-westward, for I knew
you to be a gracious and compassionate God, slow to anger,
rich in mercy, and repentant of evil. Now, then, Yahweh,
3 kindly take my life away from me, for it is better for me to
die than to live!" But Yahweh replied: "Is it right for you to
feel anger?"

At the spectacular display of repentance on the part of the Ninevites, Yahweh displays a no less extravagant *volte-face*. The "repentance" of the Ninevites, you will note, is expressed simply as a
"turning away" from their former conduct, a change of direction
from a detour into the right way. Yahweh's "repentance" on the other hand (derived from the Hebrew root *ñaḥam*) has about it the con-
notations of a profound emotional conversion, a reversal of the entire
psyche. The New Testament equivalent, *metanoia*, "change of
mind," might be thought a pale equivalent, did we not recognize that
"mind" in the ancient world meant self or identity and not merely a
chance deviation from a set course directed by some better opinion.

Contrary to Num 23:19, for example, it is being asserted here that
Yahweh can and does reverse his position, change his mind, and confound his devotees by leaving them entirely in the lurch as regards
what they have prophesied what he will and will not do.

Jonah is an antic prophet, but he is also the prophet of an antic
God. We have no reason to believe Jonah when he protests that he
knew all along that Yahweh would have pity on Nineveh and for
that cause he had fled from Yahweh's call. Jonah's attachment to the
truth is less than reliable. What his motives were for fleeing from the
divine call are forever his, and forever hidden. On the other hand,
once he had accepted the call, however reluctantly, he had the right
to be backed up by the God in whose name he was confidently pre-
dicting inexorable doom, and that within forty days.

And now, all the rules have been changed. God is not what he
was. Nothing is what it was. Life has become a frightening enigma—
an enigma to Jonah more than to others, perhaps, in view of his ambiguous precedents—but an enigma in any case. What can be said
with any certainty with regard to any God who is supposed to act in
accordance with the accepted rules of wisdom and prophecy?

Thus Jonah's appeal to Yahweh in v 3 that he die rather than
live. It is not a petulant cry of despair nor is it a fatalistic death-
wish. It is simply the assertion of a bewildered—if reluctant—servant
of the Lord who thinks that that Lord has betrayed a consistency on
which he thought that he could rely.

And Yahweh's answer (in v 4) is no consolation. "Is it right for
you to feel anger?" can be answered yes or no. Yes, Jonah has been
led up the garden path. No, Jonah should have known better. Yahweh is not kind to his chosen emissaries, and anyone who does not
understand this fact is incapable of understanding biblical history.

> 5 Then Jonah went out of the city. He sat down east of the city,
>   then made himself a hut there and sat down beneath its
> 6 shade while awaiting to see what would happen in the city.
>   Yahweh God provided for a leafy plant to spread out above
>   Jonah, to be a shade for his head and to shield it from evil.
> 7 Jonah welcomed the plant with great joy. Then, at next day's
>   dawning, God provided for a worm to attack the plant so
> 8 that it withered. When the sun rose, God provided for a burn-

ing east wind, and then the sun attacked Jonah's head so that
he became faint. He asked for death to his being, for he said:
"It is better for me to die than to live." And God said to
9 Jonah: "Is it right for you to feel anger because of the plant?"
He answered: "Right it is for me to feel anger, even to
death!"
10 Then Yahweh replied: "You are concerned about the plant,
for which you did not labor and which you did not grow,
which appeared in one night and perished in another. And
11 should I not be concerned about Nineveh the great city, in
which there are more than twelve times ten thousand people
who don't know their right hand from the left, not to mention
the many animals?"

Critics sometimes note, since v 5 has Jonah quitting the city to
see what would happen, that this verse logically should follow 3:4:
having delivered his message to Nineveh, Jonah retires to a coign of
vantage to await the predicted disaster that must occur after the pre-
scribed forty days (or, less likely, the three days of the Septuagint).
Why else the building of a hut? But on the other hand, if we extract v
5 from this present context and transfer it above, we are left with un-
answerable questions. The succeeding vv 6–11 certainly presuppose v
5, and they also seem to presuppose the whole episode of 3:10–4:4
which has preceded it. Our best judgment is that the author of Jonah
was far more interested in sending certain signals than he was in the
narrative structure of the vehicle by which he chose to send them.
Both 3:5–4:4 and 4:6–11 are logical narrative sequences following on
4:5. Narrative logic, however, is not at a premium in the Book of
Jonah.

It is more than fascinating to reflect that the "leafy plant"
which Yahweh "provided" to spread out above Jonah like a para-
sol—"leafy plant" is a non-committal rendering of whatever was the
qiqāyon of the Hebrew text—could once upon a time divide the
church of God, or at least some of God's churchmen, into opposed
camps. Back in the days when the text of the Bible was as familiar to
the ordinary concerned citizens as a daily newspaper might be today,
the correct vernacular translation of this word became an issue

which separated two eminent doctors of the Western Church, Augustine of Hippo and Jerome. The Septuagint Greek—which Augustine, like many of his contemporaries, considered to be divinely inspired and more "authentic" Scripture than the original Hebrew—had translated the word *kolokyntha,* "gourd," reproduced in turn by the *cucurbita* of the Old Latin version of the Bible (a translation of the Septuagint), and this, for Augustine, was ineluctably the "leafy plant" of Jonah. Jerome, to the contrary, was making a fresh translation into Latin of the Hebrew Bible, the translation which eventually became known as the Latin Vulgate, and along with many another rendering of far greater import he felt the Septuagint in this instance to be incorrect. He translated the Hebrew word with the Latin *hedera,* "ivy"—and Augustine charged that this was a great scandal to the faithful, who would not be asked to believe that the word of God was other than what they had been taught.[1] (Whether the fact that ivy was the vine sacred to the god Dionysius influenced Augustine's reaction does not appear from the sources.)

We are tempted to smile nowadays at such a controversy. The net effect is to cheapen rather than enhance respect for the biblical word, by confusing the trivial, the incidental, the peripheral about it with what is its real message, by making shadow and substance all one. Similar phenomena recur, however, even in our times with the appearance of any fresh vernacular translation of the Bible. This is true whatever the vernacular may be,[2] though it seems that English-speakers are peculiarly afflicted by the syndrome. Habituated, like Professor Henry Higgins, to equate "the Bible" pure and simply with the Authorised (King James) Version of 1611—the English of which, as a matter of fact, was regarded as somewhat barbarous by its contemporaries when it was first launched[3]—they not unnaturally judge translations that deviate from that norm to be aberrations. Not unnaturally, since the King James Version, for later generations, has established itself as classical English. And for some obscure reason, book review editors generally assign to the care of an English major any new translation of the Bible, rather than to someone cognizant of ancient Near Eastern culture, history, and literature, of the Hebrew and Aramaic languages, of Hellenistic and *koine* Greek, or of cognate literatures. It would probably not occur to the same editor to make a similar assignment of a fresh translation of the *Odyssey* or the *Iliad* or the *Song of Roland*.

In any case, we can view the "leafy plant" of v 6 without further distraction for what it signifies rather than attempt to define its botanical specifics. Like the great fish, it is providentially supplied for Jonah not only to shade his head from the sun but also "to shield it from evil." In context, this latter clause is probably not simply synonymous with the former. In context, Jonah is not a sympathetic character. He has retired from the city not to wait confidently on the fulfillment of the Lord's word which he has delivered, but rather "to see what would happen," and expecting the worst. The plant, therefore, also has the symbolic function of God's protection of Jonah against himself, of his trying to cure Jonah of his cynical malaise.

Yet God is antic still. Is it quite by accident that it is Yahweh God who "provides" the plant that shelters Jonah, that it is only God who "provides" the worm and the burning east wind that succeed and destroy it, while again it is Yahweh who in vv 10–11 drives home the lesson? Perhaps we are proposing subtleties that the author did not intend. At any rate, what the Lord gives gratuitously, equally gratuitously he can take back. Jonah had rejoiced at the presence of the plant, and understandably he is vexed at its sudden demise. But could any such experience justify quite this exaggerated a reaction? A sense of frustration, yes; a cry of despair, maybe; but a death-wish? And not only a passing death-wish but one confirmed and reaffirmed under direct interrogation. "Right it is for me to feel anger, even to death!"

We are in the face of another prophetic parody. Jonah appears here as a reflection of Elijah who (1 Kgs 19:4–12):

> went a day's journey into the desert, and came and sat down under a broom tree. Then he prayed for his death: "This is enough, O Yahweh, take away my life; for I am no better than my fathers." And he lay down and slept under the broom tree. . . . And then he came to a cave, where he lodged. But the word of Yahweh came to him: "Why are you here, Elijah?" . . . Then Yahweh said: "Go forth and stand upon the mountain before Yahweh, for Yahweh will

be passing by." A strong and great wind rent the mountains and broke into pieces the rocks before Yahweh, but Yahweh was not in the wind. After the wind there was an earthquake, but Yahweh was not in the earthquake. After the earthquake there was fire, but Yahweh was not in the fire. And after the fire, there was only a whisper.

This passage from 1 Kgs is already something of a parody, for it is contrasting the revelation of God made to Elijah in "a whisper" with the great theophany to Moses in thunder and lightning (somewhat like the appearance of Yahweh to Job) when Moses had to hide himself in a cleft in the rock of Mount Sinai lest he be overwhelmed by the majesty of God (Exod 19:16–25, 33:17–23). Moses, Elijah, Jonah: the varieties of prophetic experience are rehearsed in traditional terms, and in the process they are mildly, though pointedly, declared to have equal relevance or irrelevance to the real life with which the author of Jonah was concerned.

Nobody can be in any doubt as to where the final message of this book is to be found. It is the final two verses, which accomplish in a few words that for which the Book of Job requires several chapters. First, there is the easy demolition of Jonah's defenses. Particularly easy, because while Job had a semblance of "principle" on his side—a personal situation that could be extrapolated into the condition of many of his fellow human beings—Jonah is in a pet over something of almost laughable inconsequence, which in a more detached mood he would have been the first to declare laughable. A leafy plant whose ephemeral existence had shielded his brow quite by accident, totally unprovided for, now snatched away in the course of nature: unplanned in the beginning, unplanned in the conclusion. This development is an "act of God": we still use such a term in clinically legal language to refer to facts of life which are neither unfair nor unjust simply because the categories of fairness and justice do not enter into the question. Life is life, not what a theologian would like to make of life. It is life itself that has to be the paradigm of existence, not what a philosopher or theologian would prefer to impose upon it as a self-satisfying ideal.

And so the final words of Yahweh, which are not without their last whimsical thrust: "I should not be concerned about Nineveh the great city, in which there are more than twelve times ten thousand people who don't know their right hand from the left, not to mention the many animals?" God is not "just."[4] God—"life" or "nature" in a secularist vocabulary—cannot be encompassed by a human comprehension, specifically an Israelite or Jewish comprehension, of what is right and proper. His concern for the animals of Nineveh (who, after all, "did penance" like their human companions) equals his concern for the 120,000 and more who, as we would say, "don't know any better," those who are children or who act with the innocence of children—and of animals. By this designation is obviously not meant the entire population of the city: after all, it was a city upon which God had meditated a deserved doom, from which he had desisted only after its turning away from evil ways. It is not simply that the guilty are being spared for the sake of the innocent, a procedure that is not really "just," when we come right down to it, though many of us have, acknowledging it or not, had much joy from this wont of the biblical God. Nor is it simply that Yahweh is having a final go at Jonah, contrasting with Jonah's exaggerated concern over a dead plant (a concern which, in any case, was hardly disinterested) his own concern for the multitude of men and beasts whom he created and would see live and not die.

Yet it is a bit of both of these, and yet a bit more. Yahweh's concern for these heathen—and of course there is no intimation whatsoever that they have ceased to be heathen—overrides any obligation he might feel to make good on the word of his own prophet. It overrides, in the name of a common humanity of a single creator God, any prior commitments freely made which have designated one people and not others the chosen of the Lord. A Jewish author is telling Jewish men and women of his time that their God set a higher priority on that which joined them to the rest of the human race, their common creaturehood even with their most inveterate enemies, than on that which had constituted them a peculiar and distinct people who had been chosen for his own mysterious purposes. This was not a popular idea to bruit about in a postexilic Jewish community that was beginning to close in upon itself, creating—for that must be the word—a largely fictitious ethnicity out of a highly selective cultural tradition which it then proceeded to equate with the only Israel of the old desert covenant. The postexilic Judaism of Ezra and Nehemiah prevailed, of course, as the eventual restoration of the religion of Israel on the sacred land of promise, but the Book of Jonah, along with Ruth and others, remains as testimony in the Hebrew canon to a theodicy which was far more generous, not at all nationalistic, and which would have been far more congenial, we may expect, to the aspirations of a Jeremiah or a Second Isaiah.

When we say, as we have, that God is not "just," we certainly do not intend to minimize the importance of the human construct of "justice," which along with the kindred concept of "equity" must rank among the noblest accomplishments of the human community. It has determined our laws, governed our courts and our legislative deliberations. It has created great parliaments, tempered, in civilized societies, "the evil things that are in the childish hearts of kings." Yet it remains, and has to remain, only one theory, one rationale, as to how and why the universe circles and spins. As long as we have no better device, we must certainly stick with this one. Only, we must never confound it with ultimate wisdom which, if we take seriously the biblical works we have been considering, is forever closed to us in this world.

A modern authority sums up at least a part of our case:

> Law reflects but in no sense determines the moral worth of a society. A reasonably just society will reflect its values in a reasonably just law. The better the society, the less law there will be. In Heaven there will be no law and the lion will lie down with the lamb. An unjust society will reflect its values in an unjust law. The worse the society, the more law there will be. In Hell there will be nothing but law, and due process will be meticulously observed.[5]

Notes

1. Cf. Joseph A. Fitzmyer, S. J., "A Recent Roman Scriptural Controversy," *Theological Studies* 22 (1961) 426–444. Needless to say, Fitzmyer is not concerned primarily with the Augustine–Jerome correspondence and far less with the correct translation of the botanical term in Jonah 4:6, but rather with present hermeneutical issues.

2. A recent case in point is the criticism of the new *Einheitsübersetzung* ("Unity Translation") of the Bible, an officially authorized joint venture of European Catholic and Protestant German-speakers. So, for example, Curt Hohoff, "Der Junge Esel: Zur Einheitsübersetzung der Bibel," *Internationale Katholische Zeitschrift* 10 (1981) 264–275. The "junge Esel" ("young donkey") of the title is in ridicule of this version's translation of the "colt" of Mark 11:7.

3. Cf. James A. Fischer, *How To Read the Bible* (Englewood Cliffs: Prentice-Hall, 1981) 10–11.

4. Cf. Terence E. Fretheim, "Jonah and Theodicy," *Zeitschrift für die alttestamentliche Wissenschaft* 90 (1978) 227–237.

5. Grant Gilmore, "The Storrs Lectures: The Age of Anxiety," *Yale Law Journal* 84 (1975) 1022, 1044.

INDEX